SPIRIT ALLIES

SPIRIT ALLIES

ALLIES

Meet Your Team
from the Other Side

CHRISTOPHER PENCZAK

WEISERBOOKS
San Francisco, CA / Newburyport, MA

First published in 2002 by
Red Wheel/Weiser, LLC
with offices at
500 Third Street, Suite 230
San Francisco, CA 94107
www.redwheelweiser.com

ISBN-10: 1-57863-214-5
ISBN-13: 978-1-57863-214-5

Library of Congress Cataloging-in-Publication Data
    Penczak, Christopher.
        Spirit allies : Meet Your Team from the Other Side
        / Christopher Penczak.
                p. cm.
        ISBN 1-57863-214-5 (pbk. : alk. paper)
        1. Spirits. 2. Parapsychology. I. Title.
        BF1552.P46 2002
        133.9–dc21
                                        2001046898
Cover image "Ghost Executives Holding Glowing Cubes" © Charly Franklin/Getty Images/FPG
Cover design by Kathryn Sky-Peck
Interior design by Jill Feron/Feron Design
Typeset in Kennerly

TCP

10 9 8 7 6 5 4 3

CONTENTS

LIST OF FIGURES AND EXERCISES

Figures

List of Exercises

CHAPTER ONE

ENCOUNTERING SPIRITS IN THE MATERIAL WORLD

WE ARE LIVING IN THE AGE OF spirit. Feelings, intuitions, and the unseen worlds are more prominent in daily life. The New Age movement burns brightly with the torch of a new spirituality, where written dogma is replaced by actual experiences in the spirit world.

◎ MODERN SPIRITUAL EXPLORATION ◎

Individuals are now seeking their own answers through the exploration of other ideas, cultures, and religions, combining techniques and beliefs from around the world to fit within a personal cosmology.

Belief in an Immortal Spirit

At the heart of most of the ancient religions and mystic schools is the belief in the immortality of the soul, the unseen essence that animates our bodies–the true self. Some of these traditions believe the spirit returns to physical life to continue the journey, to experience, remember, learn, and ultimately live in this unique combination of body and spirit again. Other religions believe the soul moves to the next level of development, more in harmony with the creator, be it in heaven, nirvana, or other word used to describe spiritual bliss.

There are wise men and women in every culture who work with the unseen. The witches of Europe take much of their tradition from the priests and priestesses of the ancient lands of Egypt, Greece, India, and Gaul. They all speak to spirits and gods to learn the future and perform magic. Modern witches are reclaiming these traditions. Spirit work comes in any spiritual context, from Christian mystics working with patron saints to the magi of the Hebrews, like King Solomon, who were great sorcerers. All in one form or another worked with the unseen realms.

The early twentieth-century spiritualist movement, with mediums holding seances to contact the dead, usually worked in a Christian context. The modern New Age movement has supplanted it. Channelers work with ascended masters, nature spirits, and multidimensional beings from the star nations. Personal beliefs, social customs, and historical time period influence the experience of spirit work, but so many constants remain. In these constants we find the threads of truth to weave our own experiences.

Past Lives

Ordinary people are delving into the realms of hypnosis and past-life regressions. By actively participating in these explorations, recalling past lessons through triumphs and tragedies, they explore their own spirits. These techniques bring better understanding of their present life patterns and their intrinsic immortality. Individuals who have no inclination to explore spirit undergo near death experiences, or NDEs, in accidents or on operating tables. During these NDEs, their perceptions rise up and they are able to see their now lifeless bodies and hear people around them. From this point most travel through a "tunnel of light," and are greeted in some afterlife by deceased family members, angels, saints, or divine beings. However, they do not cross over, because it is "not their time" and they must return to the land of the living. They reenter their bodies and their hearts start beating again.

The experience is profound and transformative. Most who survive an NDE have no doubt about the validity of life after this mortal coil and believe that there are loving creative spirits supporting and guiding them. Many who have no previous religious beliefs become shining beacons for their community. By sharing their experience, they teach others not to fear death, to believe in the unseen realms of spirit, and to live with love and freedom.

Healing and Energy Work

Seekers are exploring alternative modes of healing and energy work when traditional medicine seems lacking. These new practitioners of ancient arts, like flower essences, Reiki, and acupuncture, to name a few, recognize the body is not just physical. Our being is a synthesis of flesh, blood, and bone with mind, memory, emotions, and energy. By affecting one aspect, you affect the whole system. Modern medical practices typically treat only the symptoms and not the root of the disease. If you have a block or imbalance in your emotional aspect, it will eventually manifest in your physical body. Likewise, emotional clearings can bring about great healing in the physical realm. Everything is interdependent.

Neopagan Communities

The amazing boom in the neopagan communities, including those that practice witchcraft, Wicca, and other Earth religions, is a mark of this spiritual quest. The children of Earth are actively searching in the material world around them for spirituality, manifested through nature and the great goddess of the planet Earth. Similarly reverent for nature are the Native American and other aboriginal traditions. The Western world is turning to the very cultures it decimated for a greater understanding of life. People are working with crystals, herbs, and ceremony for their healing and empowerment, much like their ancestors did.

◎ THE SPIRIT REALMS ◎

The common thread among these views is the belief in spirit. Spirit is the unseen force within us all. Spirit in body is called the soul. A unifying spirit, God, Goddess, or the Great Spirit, is the creative force of the universe. Quantum physicists call it the unified field or holographic universe. The name does not matter, as long as you rec-ognize it. Our individual spirits are created from the unifying spirit so it can experience itself. Many feel our spirits are embodied for this reason. If our spirits are here, there are many other spirits, in other realms, experiencing other things. If our souls are truly immortal, we can have these other experiences after this life, or now, through shamanic techniques and psychic talents.

Entire religions and complicated cosmologies are based on these other realms. Traditional Christian religions use the framework of Heaven and Hell. One realm is union with God, enlightenment, and fulfillment after a just life. The second realm is punishment and sep-aration. Purgatory is like a waiting room for souls not yet ready for Heaven, but not deserving of Hell. Destination is preordained or a result of conforming to a church's moral and ethical code, depend-ing on the sect. The concept of Heaven and Hell seems to be a dis-torted version of the tribal lore of many indigenous cultures.

Planes of Reality

Many shamanic cultures believe in a lower world of regeneration and healing, where a soul goes before its next Earthwalk. Although dark and mysterious, akin to the collective unconscious, the underworld is not a place of torment and punishment unless you create that reality. The upperworld is a city of light, contain-ing gods and heroes of myth, where insight and enlightenment are granted. We live in the middle world, the realm of linear time and space. The connecting force between the three worlds is usually a mountain or world tree.

Paradigms divide reality into the etheric, astral, mental, and emotional planes.

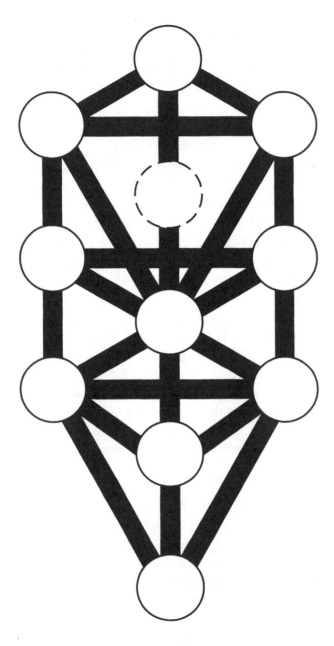

Figure 1. The Tree of Life

The Tree of Life (see figure 1 on page 5) from the Kabbalah, is a map of reality with ten sephiroths, or spheres, marking ten different realms of reality before reaching unity with God. Those in the New Age lightworker context use the word *dimension* for these other planes, or density levels, and believe each dimension is populated with many beings suited to that vibration.

Belief Systems

Any of these systems work, but the simplest view suits our purpose here, dividing reality into life in the physical world, with a body and physical matter, and life in the spiritual world. This simple system was adopted by the early twentieth-century mediums who routinely worked with the worlds beyond the veil, although its terminology is much older, perhaps dating back to the Kabbalah. Although I personally believe the universe is much more complicated than physical and nonphysical, this terminology serves our needs here and now. The material presented in this book should not conflict with most preexisting beliefs. Spirit work is not exclusive to any one religion or spiritual path. As you explore these experiences, I hope you will open to more possibilities as your experiences change. Detachment from a rigid belief system or hierarchy has been one of the greatest tools I possess, but to remain detached can be a struggle. Attachment to one way as the "right way" for everyone is a function of pure ego and can detract from spirit work.

The Veil

An invisible barrier marks the bounds of the physical realm and the spiritual world. This veil divides spirit from matter, but we are bound to both. Like an actual veil, a piece of cloth, the barrier can be easily crossed by those who know where the openings are. Spirits send messages across, and we can ask questions. Relationships, too, exist across the veil. A physical veil is also a ritual tool to block out distracting physical light so a seer or mystic can function in the spirit light. The veil is the magical blindfold, used by shamans, mystics, and witches, and it can be used to cross the barrier between worlds. Sometimes, the barrier is said to consist of many veils.

Intermediaries

All people are searching for true spirituality, but they are usually missing a direct, intimate connection to spirit. Spirituality is honoring and working with the spirit inherent in everything. Too many people are still looking for an intermediary to the unseen realms. Drilled into the collective psyche of Western culture is the need for a priest or minister to interpret the words of the gods, from the Roman Catholic pope to the priest-kings of ancient pagan lands. All have their place and can do a lot of good for the people they serve, but many modern spiritual leaders take advantage of their people's need for an intermediary. You need not look any further than the television evangelist scandals of the twentieth century. Beware of leaders who do not empower the members of their organizations, who build a cult of personality dependent on themselves or their title. This is where many religions fail us, but we can find the threads of true and honest spirituality and weave our own cloak from personal belief, understanding, and experience. A good intermediary, be it a mainstream minister or modern witch, will encourage you to make your own connections to spirit.

◎ Spirit Allies ◎

A spirit ally is a being in the unseen realms who, for whatever reason, decides to aid, befriend, protect, or teach us while we live our own Earthwalk, our time in body. They come in many forms and names, but essentially they all provide the same functions.

Allies can be with us from birth, knowing our own spirit from the other side of the veil. Central and South American medicine men believe that children will not survive the maladies and accidents of childhood without a strong spirit helper to protect and guide them. I think our own imaginary friends from childhood are not so imaginary. They are our first experiences in the spirit world. A friend's nephew vividly talks about his imaginary friend. He speaks to the shadows and the shadows, give this four-year-old some amazing insights. His parents discourage him and tell him they are not real, but we encourage him to never forget his invisible friends and to remember they are always there when needed.

Allies are also acquired through other experiences in life, particularly if we choose to pursue a more mystical vocation for our life's calling. Shamans have many spirit helpers, acquired on otherworld journeys. These allies help in rituals and healings. Native American traditions encourage a vision quest by shamans, tribal people, and modern practitioners. Individuals spend one or more nights in a secluded and sacred spot, such as a mountaintop. They prepare the area with their ritual tools, like prayer knots or arrows. Carrying their intentions in the tools, and using techniques such as fasting, isolation, darkness, or a ritual sacrament of vision-inducing herbs, they meet their spirit helpers.

Fears and Doubts

Those who fear the spirit world and their connection to it deny the fundamental truth–they are spirit in a body; they cannot escape the unseen realms. Dabblers fear they are going crazy. Cultural conditioning says they cannot be talking to something they do not see. A Native American shaman or Tibetan holy man might have visions and communications from the higher dimensions, but not an accountant, factory worker, teacher, or homemaker. Some people believe this to be brainwashing or think their own spirit work is the start of mental illness, like schizophrenia.

After having a long conversation with a friend who thought I was crazy for talking to spirits, we determined a good rule of thumb to distinguish the two. When working with spirit allies, you can turn off the experience when you want. You can consciously decide to end communication. They honor your free will and respect your intent. You set the boundaries and limits. Their advice expands your viewpoint and works with love and forgiveness. When mental illness is present, you cannot stop the experience. The messages appeal to your ego with an "us verses them" attitude. Messages are incoherent or the individuals receiving them are not in contact with the physical reality of the third dimension. They cannot take care of themselves. Although these experiences are very real to those with mental illness, they are created from a biochemical imbalance.

To my knowledge not one of my students has ever had a problem leading to any type of mental illness when contacting spirit allies. Although the modern medical establishment finds it weird to talk to someone who is not physically present, I have not known anyone to become imbalanced emotionally, mentally, or biochemcially from such experiences. They learn how to discern beneficial spirits from more mischievous or misleading ones, and such spirits are easily banished. They learn to question everything and to follow nothing blindly.

The biggest problem is the shock regarding the accuracy of the information. Some have difficulty hearing a message clearly at first. It takes practice, but the veil is closed to no one. Everyone is spirit, and everyone has a right to communication, relationships, and support from our invisible allies. The road is blocked only if you deny it and do not want to explore these realms. Your allies find other ways to contact you.

Trust Your Own Experience

Brave souls are ready to actively pursue communication, first looking to spiritual leaders, then finding their own experiences. They easily work with spirit themselves by petitioning those allies who are ready and waiting to talk to them. The techniques are simple and require no set structure of belief. You do not have to change your own religious affiliation or belief, but as you explore, your cosmology will widen to allow new experiences into your heart. You need not belong to any organization or call yourself anything different, but a dramatic transformation and empowerment is possible as you discover your spirit allies. All you need to start with is intent and the openness to experience.

Across the world and throughout time, with perhaps the exception of the modern world of reason, most cultures believe in the existence of spirits and in the possibility that many spirits have a positive impact and influence on our physical lives and spiritual quests. Even in the age of reason, and perhaps because of it, modern people are searching for answers their traditional religions and sciences fail to provide.

Our spirit allies come with many gifts. They have the benefit of another viewpoint, beyond traditional space and time and beyond traditional needs and worries. Our allies are in a closer state of unity with the source of creation, giving us unconditional love and support. Spirit guides could have lived in a body and experienced similar situations. We benefit from their wisdom. The important thing is to find spirits we know and trust, who radiate love and are interested in our highest good. Take the first step. The unseen road is waiting for you.

CHAPTER TWO

TALKING TO THE GODS WITHIN

IN AN AGE WHEN SO MANY FEEL disconnected from their own spirit, allies in the unseen realms are unthinkable. The very existence of the unseen is still under dispute by many. It is not something you can measure and define with your rulers and microscopes. But mainstream thought is starting to understand the spirit, at least in psychological terms. For instance, mainstream medicine is now acknowledging the mind and body connection, and, I hope, the mind, body, and spirit link.

Popular psychologists have rediscovered the mystery traditions, interconnections of the universe are explored with renewed interest in the works of Carl Jung and the concept of synchronicity, and the ancient alchemists' teachings of transformation are being studied. The population at large is more likely to accept the terminology and explanations of psychology, now a respected discipline, over unfamiliar mystical teachings. Because of the way individual divinity is expressed in modern culture, the idea of talking to your own inner divine aspect, your internal guide, becomes more appealing to some than the belief in spirits. You are talking to the gods within, the wiser part of you. This is but one model of spirit allies. Many more exist, and these models can all exist side by side. The seeker finds truth in many paradigms; one does not invalidate the other. Many things are occurring in spirit work. If you desire to understand the process, you will find a paradigm, or paradigms, to fit your worldview. For now, explore the concept of the divine within.

◎ ASPECTS OF YOURSELF ◎

Your own inner voice, your intuition, is your best guide. Many people never work with spirits but follow their own inner knowing, their consciousness. Through your imagination and powers of creativity, the message comes. The spirits you encounter can be part of your own consciousness, aspects of your personality.

The Anima and Animus

From the work of Carl Jung, we have the concepts of anima and animus. The anima is the feminine portion of consciousness in a physical male and the animus is the masculine part of consciousness in a physical female. Everyone contains energy of the two genders in differing amounts. The combination makes us unique. Every woman has masculine energy and every man has a feminine side. Generally, masculine is considered active and electric, yet it is often gentle and nurturing, like Jesus or Buddha. Feminine energy is receptive and magnetic, but it can be strong and fierce, like a warrior goddess. A lot of social customs deny this, but most ancient cultures knew it to be true.

Because of our social training, working with these aspects of consciousness is a part of maintaining a healthy balance. They give us a different view to any situation, usually a view we think we lack but that is inside us all along.

The animus and anima take on physical characteristics and personality in our minds. We communicate with them like spirits, because they have their own measure of independent consciousness. This does not mean you are developing multiple personality disorder. You are using the aspects within your own being. Some call them subpersonalities. We all have these parts of ourselves that remain hidden. One school of thought feels the animus and anima are mutually exclusive. Men have only an anima and women have only an animus. Other experiences show a personification for each gender. One person can meet both internal aspects. They symbolize the ideal man and woman for each of us.

When working with spirit allies, you can meet both a male and female guide together. With my first experience, I did. I assumed them to be my anima and animus. Later on, as my belief systems changed, I discovered something different about them. They allowed me to see more when I was ready. Or they changed as I changed. Perhaps all spirit allies are a form of our own consciousness, or the animus and anima may be something else entirely. As you can see already, the potential viewpoints are growing. In the end the descriptions never matter; they are all labels. When they cease to be useful, no longer use them. Either way, I appreciate all the help they have given me.

The Inner Child

For a while everyone was talking about healing the inner child. In the most roundabout ways they meant taking care of part of their consciousness, their childlike innocence and happiness. Because of many family problems, people have strong resentments and hurts from their childhood. Working with the inner child is a way to heal those pains by becoming your own parent and now giving yourself the love you needed and did not get. Give your inner child the encouragement to follow your dream if you never got it. The inner child aspect of our being is a great guide to healing and releasing past trauma. The child can lead us to issues we need to confront or it can bring us to a lot of fun.

Unfortunately, most people talk about their inner child in the abstract. The idea of visualizing and meeting this part of themselves seems silly, but they will buy expensive cars, entertainment systems, and wild trips all in the name of the inner child. Spoiling yourself when you are feeling deprived can be good therapy, but the real gift is in meeting and loving another part of you.

The Medicine Wheel

I learned the inner child aspect as part of the medicine wheel cere-mony. This version is probably a very New Age, anglicized version of it, but the ideas behind it are very powerful. In the medicine wheel, each of the four directions is connected to the four elements. Each element represents a different aspect of consciousness. Through ceremony you can meet and converse with these aspects of your own personality. Ceremonies to the four directions are common across the world.

In the medicine wheel

◎ South is the element of earth. Earth is the inner nurturer, the caretaker or inner parent. Earth is stable, being the foundation of material care and comfort. In magic, Earth deals with the body, resources, and the Earth goddess, the provider of all.

◎ The nurturer takes care of the inner child, who is in the West, with the element of water. Water is the element of healing, deeper consciousness, intuition, and emotion. The child leads to healing and a rebirth of innocence.

◎ In the North is the warrior. This inner guardian is the protector and defender of the being. It can be tough and aggressive, with weapon in hand, ready to use tooth and claw to protect. The warrior works with the element of air, the power of conscious-ness and thought, and is associated with blades and swords.

◎ And in the East is the inner spirit, the light and fire of con-sciousness. Fire is connected with the rising Sun. This is identity, life, and willpower.

All these aspects are a part of us. We each have a physical, emo-tional, mental, and spiritual side. We each are the sum of our parts, but the power of these beings within comes from our own con-sciousness. They are aids, like all spirit allies.

Inner Witness

In various combinations, these internal spirit allies make up our inner witness, the one who can look back on our life with compassion and no judgment. The witness is the part of our consciousness that can observe our rational mind, our ego, and ask it to take a break while we exist in a state of pure consciousness. The inner witness is developed in meditation disciplines, particularly from the East, like yoga. Through acknowledgment of this witness, we quiet the internal dialogue. We cease to identify solely with the body or mind and realize we are the being with the body and mind. We transcend them. We are the consciousness, or spirit, beyond them. We are the witness. Because of this transcendence, we are our own greatest ally in the spirit world.

◎ THE COLLECTIVE CONSCIOUSNESS ◎

Your *unconscious* is the deep well of knowing and understanding. We usually are barred conscious access and control of its vast power, hence the name unconscious. We are not fully aware of it. The *subconscious* lies on its surface, like the clearer waters sitting on top of a deep, murky ocean. As we intuitively collect messages from our unconscious, the subconscious dresses these communications in symbols that are floating on its surface. Through the symbols we can understand the messages we get, particularly through dreams.

Each of our personal oceans is connected to the vast sea of minds, not only of human life, but of all life. This is the *collective unconscious*. Some refer to it as the astral plane, and some feel the collective unconsciousness is but one doorway to the astral. Again, it is really a question of labels. Like the physical dimension, this is a cocreated reality where we can interact together. The rules governing the astral are more flexible than the laws of physics. Here we can interface with all forms of life, physical and nonphysical. Think of it as a common playground.

In the collective unconscious we encounter images from dreams and nightmares, from mythology and imagination. Humanity has constantly encountered repeated themes throughout its history. Now in the age of information, we have access to the mythos of the world. Many cultures have their father god, mother goddess, under-world powers guarded by strange monsters and heavenly beings in cities of glass and light. These images appear in our visions and dreams, even though the cultural context is different.

Archetypes

We all have dreams of falling uncontrollably, flying, or being some-place important in only our underwear. These repeated images are called archetypes, a term coined by Jung. Archetypes exist in the realm of the collective unconscious, to which we all have access. Only so many themes exist, but in countless variations and combi-nations. The only question is, did we collectively create them or were they always there? Maybe they had a hand in our creation. Modern shamans feel we are vessels for the archetypes.

Archetypes are not resigned to the realms of the esoteric. They originate there, but their images creep into our everyday world. Archetypes exist in everything we touch, and it is human nature to include these primal images in our daily life. Some of our spirit allies even originate as archetypes.

A popular system of archetypes is the tarot cards, containing not only the images, but also a sequence of transformation. Tarot is the journey of life and death, spiritual awakening, rebirth, and return to the cosmos. Many meditate with the card archetypes for advice on particular areas in their lives. For instance the King of Swords is a great archetype for learning the art of protection, while the Priestess brings lessons of magic.

The sacrificed king is a popular pagan theme, an archetype of the ruler dying to save his people. Dionysus was the sacrificed and res-urrected king of the ancient Greeks. He is the god of love and com-passion and of wild abandonment and frenzy. In modern mythology Jesus, the Son of God, was crucified to save all. In the ancient

Americas, Quetzalcoatl is a similar figure. Certain sects see him as Jesus after his resurrection, working with another culture.

Jim Morrison, the lead singer of a band called the Doors, was a man of great abandon and excess, a Dionysian figure. To his fans, he was demigod-like and opened the doorways of perception. He later killed himself, and speculations abound regarding a faked death and mysterious sightings. His magic still lives, and I have no doubt he embodied the sacrificed king archetype as, like many others, his story changes and mutates over time.

◎ THE HIGHER SELF ◎

If you think of your unconscious as your lower self, your deep intu-itive natural wisdom, then there is naturally a counter, or balance-a higher self. The higher self is a fully conscious and aware aspect of our being. The concept is described best through analogy. As our shadows are to our physical being, so we are to our higher selves. Our shadow is unaware of our existence. The shadow lives in a world of black, white, and gray. It cannot smell or taste. Its exis-tence is two-dimensional. Everything we do affects the shadow, where it goes and what it does.

The higher self lives in a higher plane and we shadow it. It looks to us with love and grace from a multidimensional aspect. We have difficulty understanding the higher self, just as a shadow would have difficulty understanding us. As you awaken to your spiritual heritage, you become more aware of this higher aspect, seeking its guidance and ultimately living it. This concept can be frightening if you think there is something lording over us, but it is not that way. Now that you have this information, life does not change, only your perception changes. You are more aware, but you still need to live and breathe and do things as you normally do. Decision is not taken away. The shadow is just an analogy. We are not shadows. We only lack the words to describe the higher self.

The higher self is a great ally because it has a better viewpoint.

Sometimes our unconscious intuitions and feelings are promptings from this higher self. The different aspects of personality, the anima/animus, and the inner child are ways the higher self communicates with you. The inner witness is another form of the higher self manifesting, bridging our mundane and transcendental qualities. A few practitioners experience the higher self as a complete persona unto itself, like working with any other spirit.

The information the higher self gives is very direct and simple, not mired in the subconscious symbolism of our lives. No decoder ring is necessary when working with it. I have had students who experienced great difficulty connecting to a spirit guide or totem animal, but when they connected to their higher self, the experience was a breeze. The higher self turned out to be the tiny, quiet, yet familiar voice they have always known.

We all have other bodies, besides the physical. We have etheric, emotional, and mental aspects. The highest, purest of these bodies, the divine or spiritual body, is identified with the higher self. The higher self can be called the true soul, our true essence and identity.

CHAPTER THREE

EXPLORING THE THIRTY-TWO FLAVORS OF SPIRIT

AFTER EXPLORING THE POSSIBILITY of spirits within, some receive experiences provoking thought about the independent lives of spirit allies. Your "inner" guide gives you specific information you did not possess. If it is only a part of you, how did it know? The experience can be explained as your own intuitive and psychic abilities, your higher self, but somehow that explanation never fits. Something more is occurring. Suddenly you find yourself diving into a new paradigm, a new model of thought. You ponder the existence of nonphysical beings, true independent spirits, aiding you in your journey. For some, this is the most likely explanation. They approach their allies as individuals.

◎ FORM AND SHAPE ◎

Spirits are as unique as people, coming in all shapes and sizes as far as our linear mind can understand. In all likelihood, beings on the other side of the veil probably do not have shape and form the way we perceive it. Our experiences are translated into terms we understand. Spirit allies come in familiar forms, reflecting their own nature and relationship with us, and appear as humans, animals, plants, and other earthly shapes.

Mythological themes are popular. Spirits can be perceived as light or have no appearance at all, but a specific presence or feeling is conjured when they are communicating with you. Some spirits, particularly those of the recently departed, keep their earthly shape. In some moments they look very real and physical. The astral body is molded by their former physical form. Those who stick around the material world, appearing to us as ghosts, keep their physical form because they still identify with it and not the otherworlds. The variety of forms, feelings, and methods of communication are endless. Each indicates our unique relationship with the spirits and their own development and personal choices.

Labels

Modern society needs to categorize and dissect anything to understand it. The whole needs to be broken down into small pieces to understand how it works. An experience cannot always be understood as a whole; all the little parts need to be found to understand the greater object. Labeling the parts makes things easier to understand, tackling the subject piece by piece. But, once you understand the concept as a whole, the labels drop away, no longer needed, particularly in spiritual subjects.

Labels help us with spirit work. Although it is perfectly possible to have a strong relationship with our spirit guides without any labels, we desire to understand them and fit them into our worldview.

Children have great relationships with their spirit guides. Children accept this other reality without question and continue to do so until adults tell them the experience is not real. There is no hierarchy to the realm of their spirit friends, just acceptance of the experience and its reality.

Adult minds need to know what spirits are, where they come, from and why they are here. Without answers to those questions, the whole experience is frightening or foolish. The unknown is a scary prospect. Jaunting out into the unknown by working with spirits, developing psychic powers, or working magic is like facing your greatest nightmare. You are frightened by what strangely fascinates you; by opening the doors to self-exploration, discovery, and healing, you open the door to darker emotions, like fear, anger, and pain. You experience them to release them. Then the energy held by these unwanted patterns is freed and put to good use. Otherwise they weigh you down. Those who fear falling really want to learn to fly. Spirit allies help you find your wings.

Categories

To satisfy the need to know within us, we can look at some spirits experienced by others. Spirits are grouped into different categories, based on mystical traditions and previous experiences. Your allies can be found in these groups, and you could discover new ones along the way. The groups you work with firsthand reflect your personal beliefs and current spiritual path or the paths you will soon be traveling. The categories run the gamut of beliefs, from those who work in the realms of popular psychology, unsure if spirits really exist distinct from the individual, to shamanic realms, modern witchcraft, and New Age paradigms.

Some would argue these paths are all true, and in a sense they are. If any one view helps your understanding and experience, use it, but be open to other possibilities. Sometimes spirit work is like walking into an ice-cream shop. The possibilities and combinations are endlessly fun to explore, but you find a few more suited to your tastes. There is never one "right" flavor for all ice-cream lovers. There is never one "right" spiritual answer for everyone.

All of these categories and divisions are just possibilities. In my practice, there is no dogma set in stone, applying to everyone's experience. I think the similarities between individuals and cultures are strong clues to how human beings interact with the spirit world, but I would not presume to tell anyone that my views are ultimately correct. I look to the common denominators, cutting across cultural boundaries.

While I was researching this material and speaking to others about their experiences with spirits, someone explained a complex hierarchy of spirits and otherworlds to me. The information sounded very convincing, technical, and authoritative. This person then told me who my guide was, what "group" he came from, and basically that I could stop wasting time with other explanations because this is the way it is, end of story. All "true" mystics knew this. If only it were that easy. Unfortunately, this explanation did not resonate with me. I had been working with my guides for several years at that point, and though I had many, the name he gave me did not sound familiar.

I questioned the complexity of this person's explanation, think-ing the universe much simpler. Spirit would work in a very clear and concise way. I meditated and asked for guidance. The answer I received from one of my longtime, trusted spirit allies was that we tend to make things much more complicated than they really are. It depends on how we look at it. If we look at the material world, we see land, water, and sky. People live with animals, insects, and plants. We can view this as a world where everything is unique but united, one dependent upon another, or we can choose to see only the diversity–the endless variety of life, divided by family, genus, subgenus, and species or culture, religion, and economics. My guides tell me life beyond this world is like our earthly plane. It can be child-like and simple, or complex and technical.

◎ THE GREAT SPIRIT ◎

In the exploration of spirit work, seekers feel they are speaking directly to the creator spirit, the Great Spirit, Mother-Father, God, Goddess, Tao, or Source. Whatever you choose to call the creator is perfectly acceptable. I call it the Great Spirit, for I also believe in a God and Goddess–in my faith, both the masculine and feminine are honored. The Great Spirit is the sum of their parts and more. When I invoke them, I ask for the Goddess and the God, the two who move as one in the love of the Great Spirit.

Speaking with spirit directly is not uncommon. In fact it was much more frequent for people to feel directly connected to the creative force. To many mainstream religions, such a connection is more acceptable. Many factions of Christianity are uncomfortable with the idea of spirit allies, but if you were talking to God, the conversation would be fine. Some foolishly believe they have the only direct line to God, and you have to go through them for forgiveness or healing. It simply is not so. We all commune with God. Only our methods are different.

The Principle of Mentalism from Hermetic Law teaches that we are all part of the divine mind. We are all thoughts in the mind of God; we all work perfectly together in the divine order; the universe has no spare parts. We forget that sometimes. So if I ask for a solution to a problem in my life, I can ask for help from God, but never hear God's answer directly. I could talk it over with my physical friend or a spirit ally. This friend may have the perfect solution. If the advice is offered in love and with the highest intent, is that not the will of God, the Great Spirit, made manifest? I definitely think so. We are all vehicles for spirit to work through us. If we are all part of the divine, all interconnected, and ultimately one spirit, our allies independent existence from our own conscious is no longer questioned. Nothing is truly independent.

I have a friend, a former student, who was having marriage problems. We went out one day, walking through the park, talking about them. Trying to make a decision in her life was tearing her up. My personal feeling, what I would do if I were in her place, would be to leave her husband. I tend to be very cut and dry when it comes to things like relationships. But before I realized it, I started to tell her it is all right not to make a decision. To decide to do nothing is a decision. I wondered how these words came out of my mouth; I had not planned to tell her these things. I told her what she needed to hear. It felt good. It felt right. My response did not have my own ego mixed with it. That answer did not have the arrogance that I knew what was best for her. I think for that moment I was the vehicle for spirit, be it God with a capital G, or one of our other spirit allies.

Prayer is speaking to God. Meditation is God speaking to you. That is a popular saying now, and I think the whole the approach is very balanced. I tend to seriously consider spiritual views that encourage a two-way relationship with spirit.

◎ Angels ◎

If the idea of talking with God directly is a bit too monumental, you can find vehicles of spirit through friends, family, ministers, and, of course, spirit allies. A more acceptable spiritual intermediary for many these days is an angel. The angelic forces are making a big comeback in the world of humans, from greeting cards and statues to books and television shows. Angels are believed to carry out the will of the Great Spirit, as messengers, protectors, and guides. Most people in North America today, even those not ordinarily religious or spiritually motivated, will tell you they believe in some form of angel. Like King Solomon, many people believe they have a guardian angel protecting them. I think everybody has a guardian spirit ally. If you are most comfortable with the form of an angel, your guardian will appear to you as such.

The popular image of angels is the beautiful, androgynous being with the silky gown, white feathery wings, halo, and a harp or trumpet. Some look like children or cherubs such as Cupid on Valentine's Day. Angel lore is much more complex, but most people are unaware of it. First, angels are not strictly Judeo-Christian. Many other cultures speak of heavenly angels. I used to be uncomfortable with the idea of angels, since I left much of my Catholic upbringing behind me in pursuit of more nature-based spirituality. Some of my own more recent teachers reintroduced me to the concept of angels, and now I feel much more comfortable working with their energies. In my mind I had a misguided notion of angels as the "enforcers" of mainstream religions, but they are a resource and support available for anyone. They are nondenominational.

Older mythologies divide angels into a hierarchy of groups or choirs. Each choir has a specific function and level of power. Many books, modern and ancient, detail specific forms and functions of angels, but I think it is better to ask one. At the bottom of the hier-archy, the closest to humanity, are guardian angels. Above them are the archangels.

Four archangels, associated with the four elements, are seen as the architects of this universe. Most famous is *Michael,* protector, patron of warriors, and guardian of the gates of Eden. His element is fire. *Raphael* is the angel of healing. His element is air. *Gabriel* works in the realm of water and is the messenger who came to the Virgin Mary and who gave Qur'an to Mohammed. Gabriel brings change. Last is *Uriel,* or Auriel, the angel of death. Most often depicted as feminine, Uriel leads the deceased soul to the afterlife. Uriel is the angel of earth and associated with graves. For those who do ritual and magic honoring the four directions, these four archangels can be called on for protection and aid. In this function they are named the watchtowers. Anyone can call upon them, while guardian angels are more individual and personal.

Most angels do not appear in our traditional image. Their wings are not always white–Uriel has black wings, like a raven. They can appear as wheels of fire, or have more than one face. Angels appear fearsome indeed. Large balls of colored light are a common modern image when we shed the need to relate to them through a human guise.

Many angels carry weapons, such as swords. Their jobs are not just to bring messages. Some sources credit angels as God's sol-diers. Another friend, far more schooled in Bible lore than I, tells me the majority of times you read about angels in the Old Testament, they are killing or destroying. And there is the story of Lucifer and the fallen angels. Mother Mary's angelic messenger telling her she will give birth to Jesus is a well-known story in the New Testament. In a meditation with Michael, led by a teacher of mine, the angel's flaming sword cut through my karmic ties to the past that no longer served me. The meditation prepared me for more advanced work and left me feeling free. In this case the sword and more aggressive aspects were of great benefit. My

Michael experience opened my eyes to the wonders of the angelic realm. I could no longer ignore them.

◎ ASCENDED MASTERS ◎

Instead of working with the more traditional images of angels, Earth's own group of angels and cosmic beings are available. This group is referred to as the ascended masters, a cooperative of beings who lived on Earth in physical bodies like we do, mastering their life experiences here, opening to unconditional love and a greater mastery over time-space for healing and guidance. They left the physical world and "ascended" to the spirit realms, but because of their great love for humanity, they continue to interact with us, and sometimes incarnate to aid the development of everyone.

Earth is seen as a school for angels or ascended masters. The eventual goal of all of us is to ascend to this greater mastery. Psychics and mystics encounter these beings and are given information, meditation techniques, or other mystical initiations for spiritual advancement.

Most ascended masters are associated with the Great White Brotherhood. The name sounded to me like something related to the Ku Klux Klan when I first heard about it, but nothing could be further from the truth. The group is an assembly of ascended masters from all over creation, with different functions and tasks. For many, their task is to assist the spiritual transformation of people living on Earth. Unfortunately, the very name prevents many people from taking them too seriously, thinking the group and those associated with it as racist or sexist. The term was created at the beginning of the twentieth century by ordinary people. The white symbolizes the unity of all the colors—white light is the combination of all colors. *Brotherhood* means "unity of people."

Do not let the limitations of our vocabulary poison you to something very helpful. Once you work with ascended masters, you can call them anything you think is appropriate, as long as they know what your personal code name for them is. I had some pretty silly names that worked for me until I got comfortable with the Great White Brotherhood. Many call them the master-teachers of Shamballa. They are also known as the Secret Chiefs, Illuminated Ones, or the Order of Blessed Souls. In Judaism, the masters are known as the Maggid. From the word *Maggid,* we get the root of the word *magus* or *magician.* In Sanskrit, the inner teachers are called the Agnishwattas.

Some worldly organizations including Madame Blavansky's Theosophical Society and The Golden Dawn magical lodge are said to be led by such ascended masters. Ascended masters supposedly gave Alice Bailey her information for the volumes of esoteric material she created. Encountered masters cut cultural, religious, and gender lines, but include religious icons, saints, and prophets like Quan Yin, St. Germain, Mother Mary, Simon Peter, Jesus, Thoth, Merlin, Aradia, and Kuthumi, who I'm told was both St. Francis of Assisi and Galileo in past lives. A few masters have never incarnated on Earth.

When working with ascended masters, it is important to use the discernment techniques as discussed in chapter 6. Quite often other spirits tell you they are somebody you think is important so you will listen to them. You are likely to take the voice of St. Germain more seriously than that of Mr. Joe Average who recently passed away and finds himself unable to cross the veil. Spirits with helpful messages, given in love and with the highest intent, do not need to pretend to be something they are not.

◎ DEITIES ◎

Before the dominance of the monotheistic religions, most people believed in polytheism, or many gods. Divinity was intrinsic in everything and personified in different aspects. The modern world is experiencing a resurgence of this belief. Polytheistic cultures have many similarities. They recognize some of the collective archetypes come to life. Polytheists are sometimes called pagan, meaning *people of the land*. Nature is held sacred. Unfortunately, the word *pagan* has almost become equated with being uncivilized or irreligious. Pagan gods are divided into a pantheon, a group of beings who are keepers of the natural elements and arts. They are intermediaries to the primal forces. Most pagan deities are very personal, not distant and remote like some images of more monotheistic patrons.

Each cultural pantheon usually has a mother goddess, represented by the living Earth. The planet is alive. Today she is known as Gaia, the Greek Earth goddess, but she has had other names. Her consciousness and personality are very real to those who listen. There are father gods, of both the sky and the land, like the Greek Zeus and Celtic Dagda, respectively. Some deities are embodied by the Sun, Moon, planets, and stars. Others find their voice in the oceans, lakes, rains, volcanoes, or clouds. Everything in nature has a patron deity. Some deities are supporters of the mystical arts, healers, prophets, poets, and metal workers.

For the modern mind, difficulty arises in fitting deities like this into the cosmology of universe. How do you differentiate God or Goddess with a capital G from the multitude of gods and goddesses found across the world. I can remember, in a witchcraft class, students wanting to know what the gods were exactly. No one can tell you exactly—the concepts are too abstract for our linear mind. Like everything else, many possibilities exist. Your perception of the possibilities is key.

I see the Great Spirit as a large diamond, beautiful and faceted, reflecting all the colors of the spectrum. Each face cut on the diamond is an aspect of the Great Spirit. Polytheistic cultures look at the diamond and see that within the one spirit running through everything are many faces. They focus on the facets. Monotheistic cultures are too distracted from the whole when focusing on the faces, so they choose to look at the entire diamond. Perhaps some groups just look at one particular facet and ignore the rest. Each one is correct, depending on the point of view. The important thing to

remember is that we are all facets on the diamond. We are not separate from it at all.

The actual gods and goddesses themselves have different origins.
Deities are the archetypes embodied in the natural world as an
aspect of the creative powers in the universe. If everything is alive
and contains energy, it contains a form of consciousness. Gods and
goddesses could be the living, guiding consciousness of physical
matter, be it an ocean, mountain, or planet. They are the spirits of
nature, the devas and dryads of the plant world. For example, Gaia
is the collective consciousness of this planet. Even though we feel
we are the dominant life-form, we are really just specialized cells in
her body. If we continue to do harm and act like a cancer, her own
immune system will have to remove us. We are usually not consciously aware of the cells in our own body, but Gaia is conscious
of us and loves us very much. She is asking that we live in harmony
now.

The gods with a more humanlike personality could be people
who have reached another level of reality, like the ascended masters. Many ascended masters are seen as gods because they are in
harmony with the creative force. Part of their new learning is to
work with the natural elements to aid humanity. They may be
avatars, celestial beings who choose to take human form to teach
and heal. Many consider Jesus and Buddha avatars. Aradia of the
Italian Strega witches is considered an avatar of the Great Goddess.

◎ ANCESTORS ◎

Honoring those who have gone before you is a tradition found
across the world, from Asia to Europe and the Americas.
Ancestors are honored because they are spirits on the other side
who take an active interest in our lives. They are connected to us.
Some are connected through blood and genetics, even though we
may have never seen them while they lived. Those who go before
us are not only our family, but anyone on our spiritual path. I

consider many of the witches from the past my ancestors, since that is the path I am on now. I also consider many of the masters in the Reiki tradition to be in my extended spiritual family, since I walk that path as well. Some take their Reiki lineage, tracing their link back to the modern founder, Dr. Usui, more seriously than their actual blood lineage.

Ancestors unrelated by blood are kindreds, those people with a similar path, problems, or inspirations as you. They have sympathy for your life and times. Think about those in the past with whom you feel a kinship. If you are a writer, you could feel a bond with a particularly inspiring author from history. Find your kindreds.

A loved one who has passed on, communicating with you from beyond is a comforting thought. People seek this communication in seances and from mediums and channels. However, you should be wary of those spirits who have not crossed to the next phase of life. Ghosts and apparitions do not seem to know any more of the secrets of life than the living. Their perspective has not changed, only their body has ceased. They are still in the physical realm. Those ancestors in the next realm often come back in dreams, visions, or feelings of comfort to advise those they left behind. They are true allies.

When my Great Aunt Mary passed away, I swear I saw her ghost in the window reflection telling me everything was okay. At the time I was fifteen, sitting in high school homeroom utterly stunned. I was not exploring anything psychic or occult at the time. In fact, I was on the verge of giving up any belief in God or the afterlife. I was going to be a man of science and reason. Her little visit changed my whole life.

My mother definitely feels the presence of her departed mother, especially when she is cooking. My grandmother loved the kitchen and telling her daughter how to cook. She still does.

When my paternal grandmother departed, many years after her husband, a painting he had commissioned of me fell right off the mantle in our home the night she died. The painting had never fallen before and has not since. I think that was Grandpa's way of telling us that she was with him now. In fact, my family joked that since they often fought, he was not too happy about seeing his wife again. I think they are happy now. Many shamanic practitioners indicate they have a closer relationship to deceased relatives than they ever did in the physical world. The change in perspective can transform a whole relationship.

Altars and shrines are established in honor of ancestors and kindred spirits, with photos, sacred objects, and food offerings. Practitioners sometimes fear certain ancestors will not respond to their call. That is a risk you run when calling any specific spirit, but we all have higher aspects that answer the call, if not with what we want, with what we need. The ancestors called on might not be "home" because they are on another mission, guiding another. They could be incarnated in another body or they know you need to be alone during a certain task. Usually, their highest aspect will answer, even if they are somewhere else.

Practitioners also fear the ancestor will not approve of the "new" spiritual path because they wouldn't have approved in life. I've heard many times new witches thinking their departed loved ones are angry because they do not follow the family's traditional faith. Once a being crosses over the veil, he or she realizes the truth to spirituality more than we could while incarnated.

All paths lead back to the top of the mountain, sooner or later. Those beyond the veil take no previous religious prejudices with them. Those are of the ego and are shed upon death. They want what is best for you, your highest good. Overall, I have found ancestors very receptive to rekindling the relationship.

◎ SOUL GROUPS ◎

Souls travel together in groups. Each group has a specific bond and combined lessons to learn. All in the group know each other well, and they incarnate on the planet in different roles. They are family, lovers, friends, or enemies on Earth. They play these games in order to experience different ways of being and learn the lessons of life. This group of souls is most like a family.

Monads

The connection among the group of souls could be caused if they were from the same monad. A monad, as described to me, is a por-tion of light from the creator spirit through which souls manifest. The monad, the divine spark, is the first separation from the creator. Each monad desires to experience different situations, so it mani-fests many souls. The souls desire a physical vehicle for experience and can manifest soul extension to incarnate in a body. Souls who come from the same monad come from the same spark. For those interested in the math, it is said each monad creates twelve souls and each soul creates twelve soul extensions, giving each monad an extended family of 144 individuals. The monad is a higher, divine presence, much like connecting to an individual's higher self. You could say the monad is to the higher self as the higher self is to the physical self. Souls from the same monad are bonded because they come from the same place, the same core family. What most mod-ern mystics think of as souls would really be soul extensions in this paradigm.

Karma

The soul family works together to clear karma. Many people think karma is the law of return: You do something bad and something similarly bad happens to you; you do something good and you will be rewarded. But karma is far more. To me, karma is love. We love ourselves so much that we want to experience everything. On a higher level, a difficult happening is not punishment, though it may seem to be when we are in a body. It is experience. We attract what we send out. It returns to us, in this lifetime or another. When we are finished with these types of experiences, we no longer need karma.

The soul family can be created by our karma. That love through experience is the binding link between its members, or as a group we have collective karma to experience and work out while we are together.

Contracts with Our Soul Group

New Age mystic teaching say we make contracts with these souls in our soul group and other souls we encounter. These contracts spell out what we agree to experience and how we will interact with the beings who play an important role in our life. Some of our soul family will stay on the other side of the veil, agreeing to guide us and support us while on our Earthwalk. Their help is part of our contract with them. They help us with the details needed to bring members of the same soul family together. They are the little nudge we feel to pick up and move to California where we meet our future husband. They know it is not easy to be in a body because the have been there before. They might have faced similar situations and are better able to support you.

Soul Mate

Opinions vary as to the definition and validity of a soul mate. The soul mate is the one who is closest to you in your greater soul family, the spirit you are most bonded to and your destined companion. This definition could be accurate, but so many people spend their lives searching for their soul mate, this perfect ideal, and never enjoy the rest of their life.

As a culture, we have a very romantic notion of a soul mate. Note that it is not called a romantic mate, but a soul mate. The bond is often on a spiritual level and not a romantic one. Your soul mate can be your very best friend. The mate might be much older or younger than you. You may not be "destined" to be together in a happy marriage in this life, but that does not mean you are not destined to have a happy marriage in this life at all. You could have loving past-life connections to this spouse in strong, spiritual, intimate ways, but the reality of the situation does not live up to what you think a soul mate should be. Nothing is perfect on the material plane. Your relationship can be great and romantic, but you just might not be with your idealized soul mate.

Your spiritual mate could be off having other experiences on the other side of the world or not in a body. Your soul mate can act as a spirit guide, across the veil. She might not be on Earth, but you can have wonderful experiences with her in your dreams and meditations. Your divine aspects, your higher selves are never separated. Unfortunately such solace never helped the disenchanted romantic.

Reincarnation

This view of spirit allies is difficult for those who do not believe in any form of reincarnation. However, if you have gotten this far, you probably believe in the possibility of consciousness beyond death. Problems with reincarnation come with believing in a hierarchical structure of soul contracts, karmic boards, and any system with levels of progression. Is coming back as a bug a punishment? Is being a monk in Tibet a reward? Karma is love and experience. It has no value judgment unless you place one on it.

How can fifty people claim to be Cleopatra, Napoleon, or Joan of Arc? As multidimensional beings, we have energy on many different levels. When we die, part of our energy, our spirit or soul, goes on to its next life, be it a physical life or in another realm. Other parts of our energy stay on Earth, like the energy in our body. It gets broken up and recycled like the molecules in our flesh and bones, which eventually decompose and become one with the land. The energy and matter get redistributed, and no one can say where it ends up. Part of the energy making up your body, or your astral body, might have once been a part of Cleopatra. When accessing past-life information, we have access not only to our soul, but the whole energy field, including our cellular memory. It could serve your highest good to think back on that time and identify with Cleopatra. No one can judge who the real Cleopatra is now, and no one can tell you your experience is not valid.

It is equally possible Cleopatra's soul has divided like a single cell, creating many souls traceable back to the Egyptian Queen. The possibilities are endless. In my own past-life exploration, I have found it important to trust my first instinct and go with it. The more I try to recall history lessons or make them match my expectations, the less information I get. Research can always be done afterward. Hypnotherapists and those specializing in past-life work are easily found now in most major cities.

◎ POWER ANIMALS ◎

Just as many Western religions believe everyone has a guardian angel, many indigenous, tribal cultures, working from the shamanic context, believe everyone has a power animal or totem. Maladies and misfortunes in these tribes are attributed to loss of power by offend-ing your power animal through neglect or dishonor. Those with good luck, success, and health are keeping their power animals happy.

Oversouls

Power animals are archetypal. Usually they are not referred to indi-vidually, but collectively. Your totem is not a raven, but Raven. But in my experience, some of them have individual names. I have recently heard that animals used to have something called an over-soul, one giant soul animating a particular species. Now they have been rewarded with individual souls. I am not sure I believe this in the way it was explained to me. Most animals in my life definitely have their own personality and individual quirks—think of the pets in your life. But I do think all our individual souls are in a similar rela-tionship with the creator. We are all individual sparks. Each species, humanity included, is linked. We share a similar consciousness.

Animal Medicine

Each animal brings to people something Native American tradi-tions call animal medicine. The animals' own physical traits bring spiritual lessons. Their natural instincts teach us things we have forgotten. Totem animals we encounter in visions and dreams come to teach us these lessons. These lessons are usually about qualities missing in our lives. Dog brings the qualities of loyalty. Coyote is the trickster, "tricking" us into seeing things as they truly are. Bear brings introspection, like the meditative hibernations. Dragonfly, with its iridescent wings, breaks illusions, and Ant teaches collective consciousness for the good of the group. Spider works with creativity and language. Mosquito deals with annoy-ance and ultimately fear. Some practitioners of the animal arts shy away from insects, but I think their medicine and lessons truly need to be reclaimed.

These totems guide and protect us in our waking and sleeping visions. Shamanic journeyers are greeted by a power animal that has a lesson for them. Shamans from the Central American tradi-tions call their totem their nagual or nahvalli. Siberian shamans call them tutelary spirits. European witches work with animal familiars.

The power animals could be the animal archetype, or original animal oversoul, but individual animals play a role in guidance. Some people are greeted by deceased pets in vision quests or feel a current pet is an old soul they have known before, here to protect or comfort them.

◎ DISCARNATE BEINGS ◎

Individuals expire physically, but get trapped between worlds, not alive, but not past the veil. People who deny and fear death, or those who die with thoughts of revenge or somehow feel their work is unfinished, remain bound to the material plane. Their willpower keeps them here. They become the ghosts popularized in stories, legends, and movies. Their knowledge and viewpoint are not any different from ours, and in fact may be less helpful, since darker emotions keep them bound. Many lose coherence and become the addle-brained dead. No communication is possible.

Some become the broken records of the ethers, with no real con-sciousness, constantly replaying a scene or two from the past.

Discarnate spirits sometimes understand their predicament, but not how to get out of it. They lie and pretend to be something they are not, but their guidance appeals to the ego, not the heart. The key out of their purgatory is love and acceptance. If they had that to offer, they would not be stuck. As a rule, they do not make good spirit allies, but you could find one who is good company. Try to help them if you can.

If you are dealing with one of these beings, ask him to go into the light. This sounds like a line from a bad movie, but there is truth in it. Visualize white light and offer it as a portal out. Light white candles and do invocations to the creator spirit in whatever faith you believe. High vibrational incense, like sage or frankincense and myrrh, help dispel discarnate beings. Laughter is a great banishment. If you cease to take them seriously, they will look for one who does, as they get bored easily. They do have a choice—they can stay on this plane, but they do not have to stay in your house to do it. Do not force them into the light if they do not want to go. Invoke your own spirit allies to help them if they do want to leave now.

Other discarnate beings do cross the veil. They may not have had a physical life here on Earth. They are not associated with any group or religion. They are not ascended masters, goddesses, or your own ancestors, but their viewpoint can be beneficial.

It is up to you to determine the intent and validity of discarnate beings. Some honestly wish to help, but have no information to give. Others do not fit our traditional, yet limited viewpoints, but come in love and wisdom. Many are only curious about us.

◎ INTERDIMENSIONAL BEINGS ◎

The universe has many realms in it. Imagine a large house, a giant mansion where you could never possibly explore all the rooms. Each floor is a different level or dimension, and each room is a place or planet. There are beings who have never been to the room Earth and have not even reached the floor representing physical life. We are all living in such a mansion. We have the potential to travel from floor to floor, room to room–to be interdimensional beings. Sometimes our room is so big we forget there are other rooms. Beings can yell down the stairs or the heating vents. We can yell out to them. When we dream, we sleepwalk to these other rooms, but always end up back in room Earth before we wake.

Much of the channeled information being published today both in books and on the Internet comes from interdimensional beings. The sources are often extraterrestrial in origin, "space brothers and sisters" from the Star Nations like the Pleiadies, Sirius, Andromeda, and Arcturus. There seems to be a joint group of these beings called the Galactic Federation. This sounds a bit like *Star Trek* to me, but the translation was probably named in a way we could understand. These beings suffer the same problem with public relations and our limited vocabulary as the Great White Brotherhood. In fact, many say the two are connected. We are the *Star Trek* and *Star Wars* generation and put the ideas of alien life in science fiction terms. Extraterrestrial life can reside in different dimensions and not have green skin or bug eyes or even be remotely physical. Many are not so much space aliens, but time aliens. Do not let names hang you up. Remember that even though someone has a different room in the house, it does not mean her view is any better for us.

◎ ELEMENTALS ◎

Elementals are the consciousness residing in the elemental planes. Each plane embodies a force and energy represented by a physical element. We have already met the archangels of the elements, who possibly created or rule the realms, but many beings work in the elemental planes. Like the archangels, they are called upon in ritual and meditation for aid and manifestation.

The traditional elements of Western magic are earth, water, air, and fire.

◎ Earth is the physical and etheric realms, containing shape and form. Earth builds the body, health, home, and finances. Material issues are from earth.

◎ Water is the astral and emotional realms, the home of the deep unconscious and love. Our intuitive connections and relationships are ruled by water.

◎ Air is the province of the mind and mental planes. We communicate, think, and observe with our airy aspect. This is the element of ideas.

◎ Fire is our spark of spirit and will. It is creative energy, passion, and sexuality in action.

All four elements are needed to manifest a wish or do magic. From the spark of inspiration, the idea takes form in the mental realm. It takes form in the astral and finally manifests in our life.

Some systems use the fifth element of spirit, or *akasha*, unifying all. Chinese mysticism has five elements: earth, water, fire, metal, and wood. Celtic mythology uses clouds and flowers as elements too. Here we are primarily concerned with the four-element system.

Elemental Shapes

Each elemental takes a different shape. Kings and queens exist in these realms, following each element's natural order. The kings are named after the four Greek winds. Elementals appear as lights, or beings composed of their elements, like a man of fire. Other images come from mythology.

◎ Earth elementals look like gnomes or dwarves.

◎ Air elementals are called sylphs and look like fairies with gossamer wings.

◎ Fire elementals are salamanders, manifesting as tiny red lizards in our mind's eye.

◎ Water elementals are undines and look like mermaids or mermen.

Elementals As Guides

Elementals can act as guides and guardians in the spirit world. You must be careful because their view will always be tempered by their nature. Earth elementals will always be practical, even in matters of the heart; air spirits will have you reason things out instead of following intuition; water elementals throw reason and practicality out to follow feelings. Because of your own personal elemental nature and balance, you may be tempted to follow one path more than the others, but decide if the path is right for you now. Always seek balance among the elements.

Elementals go through a learning cycle like we do, but without the aid of reincarnation, and they develop more complexity and understanding of their patterns. They travel from element to element, mastering each aspect. When they master all four, some speculate they become angels, dragons, or human souls.

◎ DEVAS AND NATURE SPIRITS ◎

Elementals are confused with devas and nature spirits, which are also aspects of the consciousness of the material world. Practitioners do not always distinguish between the two, but in general, devas hold the patterns and forms for the world. Nature spirits actually build and grow into the pattern provided by the deva. Nature spirits are very much like elementals, but work with a combination of elements, not just one. Perhaps when an elemental masters more than one element, it becomes a nature spirit. The pagan god Pan is considered to be the omnipresent nature spirit all over Earth. Devas and nature spirits are in perfect partnership and cooperation. The deva of oak trees provides the pattern of the tree, but the spirit that grows into the individual oak tree is the nature spirit, bringing the oak into physical reality.

All plants, trees, and minerals have devas and nature spirits. Areas of land, like yards, parks, and mountains have devas. Even office buildings and companies can have devas. If there is structure and form governing something, it probably has a deva that helped it along.

Working with the devas and nature spirits can be most helpful. For those working with natural forces, like flower essences, crystal healing, herbalism, and cocreative gardening, it is necessary. Any of the books by Machaelle Small Wright and Perelandra, like the *Perelandra Garden Workbook*, are a great resource for working with devas and nature spirits. They pioneered much of the modern information we have.

◎ INCARNATE BEINGS ◎

Some of our best spirit allies are right here with us on Earth. They are the people in our family or circle of friends whom we know on the other side of the veil. We make each other comfortable and support each other in these times. These spirits incarnate with us so we are not alone in the material world. We are all old friends working out our issues, but celebrating the good times together. Pets can be incarnated spirit allies, bringing support, lessons, and unconditional love in a physical form.

Our own guides may work through our loved ones, giving them the right words we need to hear or things to do. We may be fulfilling the same function in someone else's life. Some guides, angels, and ascended masters precipitate a body, or the illusion of a body, when needed, bring a physical form to our world, come in and do their work, and leave without a physical trace. Accident victims report being pushed out of the way of certain death by a stranger, their guardian angel, who mysteriously vanishes before anyone can question him.

The higher selves of physically incarnated people can act as spirit guides. A teacher of mine unknowingly appeared to a stranger in crisis, in his fever dreams. Being something of a local celebrity, she was easily found by this man formerly in crisis who told his tale. She surmised her higher aspect was acting as a guide. One of my students met a guide of a long-lost family member and assumed it to be his ancestor spirit. Later, he discovered this relative, while very old, was still alive. Our higher self does many tasks we are not consciously aware of doing.

◎ CONSTRUCTS ◎

Construct spirits are those that have been made by a human. They are constructed from personal power and the energy available all around us. Constructs are created through the use of a thought-form. Through will, intent, visualization, and often ritual, an energy form is created. This is like the skeleton of the spirit. This form is then imprinted with a set of instructions. Simple instructions for thoughtforms are used in creative visualization and ritual magic. Witches and magicians know this strategy well. If your desire is to get a job you like, the thoughtform is programmed by your intent and visualization with the instructions to get and manifest for you a job you like. The more complicated the instructions, the harder time the construct has. You can stipulate that the job have a certain pay scale, but that narrows the range of jobs available. The construct goes out into the universe and reflects back what you need. That is all the energy it has, and when the construct accomplishes its goal it returns to its basic energetic components.

Advanced practitioners of the magical arts create complex, semi-permanent thoughtforms. They are called servitor spirits, though the name is deceiving. They are not bound against their will. Constructs are more like spiritual machines or engines running on our intent. The instructions can be for a general function, like protection, but complex enough to adapt to the new stimulus. Magical wards and protection shields around homes use this technique. By reinforcing the visualization and intent, or more importantly, recognizing and thanking it, you are feeding this new spirit new energy to keep the motor going.

Some constructs are not intentionally created. Everyone has thoughts and creates thoughtforms all day. The universe works on exchanges of intent and energy. Even if you do not do magic or creative visualization, you can still send your thoughts out and have them reflected back on you. Some thoughts, particularly those we would call negative or harmful, build into powerful thoughtforms the more we repeat them. Then they get trapped in our personal energy and aura, replaying these unwanted messages over and over again. If your mantra at work is "I hate my job," the thoughtform is going to stick. Even when better opportunities come along or things get easier, you will not take advantage, because you have programmed your thoughtform to hate your job. That is all you reflect back to yourself.

Thoughtforms from other people can latch on to us, absorbing and magnifying whatever we are sending out. Some intentionally created constructs are forgotten like stray cats and have to find a new source of food. This new source is unknowingly feeding it energy. The construct takes a new program and latches on to its source of nourishment. From here we have many roots of spiritual sickness and concepts of energy-draining vampires or little demons putting bad thoughts into our heads. Most of them are of our own creation, or we have attracted them to us through our lifestyle. They can be removed through a beneficial change in lifestyle, including diet, exercise, and meditation, through creative visualization, or with the help of a skilled healer and psychic.

◎ Bound Spirits ◎

A bound spirit may fit any of the descriptions above, but it is bound to the service of another. Some may willingly agree to such contracts on a spiritual level, but some are coerced. Binding spirits is an old skill used by some of the more ignorant magicians and mystics, forcing their will on another spirit. Many of our stories of bound demons or djinns trapped in a lamp, carrying out another's will, come from this belief. Certain spirits are constructs created by others, changed and chained to the mage's will or the spirits of the recently dead who stay in darkness and fear. I have heard of people forcing elementals and nature spirits to carry out their plans, offering them no respect or courtesy.

A true mage knows to work with only those who want to work with you. There is plenty of help out there. A polite invitation is the only requirement. You must honor and respect all spirits who aid you. As a general rule, the higher, so to speak, a being is on the spiritual ladder, the less likely it can be bound. Free will is the rule of this universe, and if one is bound, on some level it is learning something, but it still does not make it right for you to do it. On a higher level, karmically you are asking to be bound yourself, to experience the other end of the spectrum. The higher guides, totems, and light beings never seem to be bound because they know they are sovereign in their own free will.

CHAPTER FOUR

PLAYING
WITH THE TEAM

EVERYBODY ON THIS PLANET HAS a spiritual support team. This group is our backup in the game of life. Entering the material world is like taking on a deadly mission for the CIA or MI-6. Pretend you are the next James Bond. You come in with certain assets and talents from previous missions, but are placed in situations out of your element. But you are not alone in your mission. You have backup. Someone will brief you on your mission, outline your goals, and warn you of the pitfalls. Another person, Q in the James Bond movies, gives you your equipment. He explains all the special things you can do. You will meet up with other agents in the field who will pass new information and orders to you. Some agents are seen and others remain in the shadows, secretly sending you codes. As you continue your career, you make your own contacts with other agents and agencies. You can communicate to headquarters through special equipment, focusing on frequencies only you and your team know. You have special codes and signals worked out. They are there for you. Without them, your mission is much harder.

In the real world, our team is made up of our spirit allies. We come into the world with this team, and build on it through our spiritual practices and experiences. We build our team and it changes as we change our beliefs. Those deeper on the spiritual path, with active, daily pursuit, will attract more allies, just as

Native Americans believe that although everyone has a spirit ally of some type, shamans have more. If you pursue spirit allies and wish to complete your life goals, more allies will come because you are helping them complete their goals. The relationship works both ways.

A lot of the Native American spirits are making themselves known to seekers living in the Americas, regardless of genetic background. Spirits who lived as shamans and medicine men are teaching their wisdom by becoming spirit guides.

◎ THE SPIRITUAL SUPPORT TEAM ◎

The spiritual support team contains many roles. Spirits can come from any of the groups explored in the previous chapters. Their roles, however, are more defined and are not mutually exclusive. You might find one ally performing many roles at once or have a very large and highly specialized team, where each ally has a single function and never works beyond that realm. Allies also change roles as we progress in our development.

Norse and Germanic shamans, as well as those from other traditions, do not differentiate between the types of allies. Their *fetch,* or spirit ally, although living independently, contains many aspects. This spirit appears in the familiar anima/animus role of a guide, but also comes as a fetch animal or geometric shape. The fetch uses whatever aspect is needed for guidance.

The Guide

The first and most popular spirit is the guide. This ally comes to help us through life's tough transitions. The guide is really our first spirit friend, one who talks to us on an equal level. Once we open the lines of communication with our spirit guide, we can talk about our issues and their solutions. Guides offer powerful, life-changing advice. Be prepared to hear the answers to the questions you ask.

Guides are an opportunity for you to simply talk out your day and share with someone if you have difficulty talking to those around you. Like a good friend they will not offer solutions if not asked, preferring you to figure it out on your own. Guides do offer encouragement, though. They are there to help you find the way. Guides are not a replacement for human contact and will encourage you to make new friends and meet new people. They want you to explore your life fully.

Not only are guides for spiritual and emotional support, but they are available for professional support and simple conversation. Many guides appear when I am doing a tarot reading for someone, giving me new information or pointing out things my conscious mind missed when explaining the cards. Other guides aid me in healing work. I see and feel them working next to me during a Reiki session. Guides help me in the classes I teach, urging me to cover a topic I normally would not cover because it fits the immediate needs of someone in the class.

These guiding spirits are readily available for simple discourse, giving direct information on somewhat spiritual topics, like explaining the human chakra system, herbalism, or hermetic philosophy. For those who think they are simply talking to themselves, these conversations will open your eyes. You will be amazed at how much information you can get from a guide on a topic you never studied. Then find a book on it and things will all fall into place. The information from your guide is correct, but they usually expand on the subject. If you are simply having an internal dialogue, how would you know such specific facts and concepts?

Power Animals

Everyone has a power animal, a primal animal spirit working with us. Those who work extensively with animal spirits tell me we each have nine totems teaching us lessons at any time. The number 9 corresponds to the sacred directions, North, South, East, and West along with left, right, above, below, and center. Some move on to make room for new animals, but we have nine whether we are consciously aware or not. Each of us has a prime power animal. Tribes were often associated with one animal. The Celtic Catti tribe worked with the feline spirit, and the cat influenced their culture, artwork, and customs. Taking direction for the main totem, other animals come into our lives. Some come for only a day, while others stick around for a lifetime. Even if we learn their lessons, they stay with us because we resonate together. The Cat spirit wants to stay with those who honor its vibration. Animal medicine lessons never truly end. They expand as we expand.

Recovery of lost or discarded power animals is an authentic shamanic healing technique. The power animal rules over our vital energy, or prana, aiding in our physical, instinctual existence. Restoring our link to a power animal restores our link to our own primal, vital, animal nature.

We forget we are animals. I do not mean that in a derogatory way. I regard animals as great and wise beings. They follow their instincts without hesitation, treat others equally, and live in harmony with creation. We have forgotten much of that instinctual wisdom. We must balance our minds and hearts with our animal nature. Animals are the great teachers of this world and their lessons are as powerful and diverse as life itself.

Power animals subtly teach us life lessons and instincts, but specifically guide us on meditative journeys through the primordial realms. They ask us to symbolically face our fears and demons. They guard and protect, but we do the work. They aid in all forms of magic and shamanism, for our own benefit and when working with others.

Guardians

Doing security detail in our spiritual support team is the guardian. A guardian is any ally invoked for protection. The main criteria are that they have power and province over the physical to protect your body. Guardians protect our entire being, the physical along with the emotion, astral, mental, and spiritual bodies. Icelandic mages call these beings *vördhr,* or wardens. If the guardian has no power in the physical, then your flesh and blood can still get hurt.

Pagan gods and goddesses, ruling aspects of nature, appear as guardians, among other things. Many gods are called on for protection. They do not have to be from pagan mythology. Jesus Christ or Buddha can be called on for protection. Jesus is particularly powerful for banishing harmful spirits. Also, because Hebrew is a sacred, power language, speaking it can move energy. Any of the Hebrew names for God, like Yahweh, Jehovah, Shekena, or Adoni, can be called out for protection.

Guides and power animals serve as guardians. More traditional guardian allies are our guardian angels. Everyone has one. Angels need to be asked for help to maximize their protective skills, since they, like other allies, do not interfere with free will. Allies do not stop the games we play. You do not need to know their name; simply ask your guardian angel or spirit to protect you in times of danger. Recently my group was doing a ritual involving angels, everyone in the group commented that they felt or saw the presence of everyone else's guardian angels circling us.

The Higher Self

As everyone has a guardian or guardian angel, everyone has a higher self. The teaching of all religions, at the core, is that we are all divine beings. The path is to remember our divinity. We are all being challenged to live with our higher self more fully in the world and not be dragged down by harmful thoughts and emotions. That doesn't mean we suppress them. We acknowledge them, work through them, and move on. Anger, hate, jealousy, and resentment should never be held or ignored, but honored.

The higher self is the prime director of your spiritual support team. From this chief spirit ally, all others take their cue. No one but you knows what is best for you. If you invoke your higher self and ask your intentions to be correct and for your highest good, you are asking that things be worked into your own grand design. As cocreators, our soul, our higher self, chose all the variables, our bodies,

parents, family, friends, situations. They are all perfect for our mission here; they are not random circumstances. Your higher self is in
partnership with the Great Spirit. It makes no mistakes for you.
Other spiritual beings on your team can have a different opinion.
They guide you, but ideally your higher self has the final approval
on everything. Allies are in constant communion with your higher
aspect.

The more in alignment with your higher self you are, the easier
things become. The world flows with you. Agonizing choices
between extremes are a thing of the past. The right doors open. You
still have challenges and face difficult circumstances, but you know
its your path and have a great conscious power to change your path
to your liking. You are doing your dharma, your life's work.

The Shadow

Some consider the shadow self to be the lower self or psychic self,
balancing the higher self, with no stigma or testing associated with
it. Other traditions consider the shadow to be the antithesis of the
Holy Guardian Angel or Higher Self, as an accumulation of all our
"negative karma" or misdeeds. Also known as the Dweller on the
Threshold, it must be confronted and defeated before deeper spiritual enlightenment can occur. Personally, I see the shadow as part
of our lower, psychic, and instinctive self, but it's the part of our
power and ability that we fear and disassociate from. It is all the
thoughts, feelings, and abilities we repress. It is a part of our
unclaimed personal power. To go deeper with your spirituality, you
must recognize it, forgive it and yourself, and integrate it better into
your own self-image. The shadow can have many layers, and you
will develop a relationship with it on deeper levels as your own
awareness expands.

Material Spirits

The last major component of your team is material spirits. These
allies are devas, nature spirits, elementals, or the consciousness of
your own body. These spirits rule in the material, physical world,

but sometimes lack higher consciousness to guide their powers. They follow your instructions and programming. Most people are unaware of these spirits and let their own stray thoughts command these allies.

The material spirits have power over your body and health. Everyone has a deva that forms the structure of their body. Everyone has nature spirits to fill out the form. Our entire body, from major organs to individual cells and the DNA within, is conscious. If you continually tell yourself you feel like a mess, your body will give you a mess. The body listens to every word of our internal dialogue. Positive affirmations are a way to counter this habitual programming. Tell your body you feel healthy, balanced, and beautiful. Reality follows thought. You are what you eat, but more importantly you are what you think.

Material spirits have power over our resources, like prosperity, career, and home. We have guides who help us formulate the best goals and career decisions. Houses and apartments have acquired their own presence, created by the family living in them. The energy and spirit there are usually marshaled into magic for home protection, health, and happiness. If you keep the home happy, it will help keep you happy. Elementals and spirits are called on in ritual magic to make intentions manifest in the material plane.

◎ TEAMWORK ◎

Spirit allies will take various forms and roles for your benefit. Allies may be very fluid, changing as you change. There is no deception in this. We simply see them in the forms most comfortable or needed, as indicated by our subconscious. Spirit is free form. All beings past this side of the many veils are in touch with their multidimensional nature. The duty of our guides is to reawaken us to our own multidimensional existence. Part of each of us lives beyond the veils. Allies support us by opening new doorways in our consciousness.

As you work with the team, you discover each ally has very individual traits. Each has a specific personality. Each has an identity. These vibrations are recognized, either through their voice if you are clairaudient, or simply by their presence, even if you see no image of them. They have a unique energy signature to tune in to, and you are one of the few people who has a direct line to them.

Position of the Players

Often you can feel allies are in a particular space around you. Those individuals with many spirit allies are at times adamant about where the guide is, to their left, right, above them, below them, or off to the side. Guides seem to be whispering into the left ear or the right. The side of the body they appear on gives insight into the lessons they share. The left side is controlled by the right side of the brain, which is more creative and intuitive and usually regarded as more feminine. Many guides work through these traits, since intuition and psychic powers go hand in hand. The left half of the brain controls the right side of the body. The characteristics considered more masculine, like logic, reason, and aggression are part of the left side. Esoterically, we usually project energy from the right hand and receive energy from the left, unless we are left-handed. Once you understand the flow of energy, you can control the flow of energy from each hand and reverse it as needed.

If a guide appears lower to the ground or off to the side, it is probably working with grounding issues, health, and being comfortable in the physical realm and in your body. You need support and strength. When the guide is floating above your head, you are working with the mind and perception.

Size of the Team

The spiritual support team varies in size from person to person, being as few as one or as many as several dozen. When there is only one, that ally fills all the tasks in the entire team and tends to be a very versatile spirit. The larger teams bring specialization, with one spirit having expertise in a particular topic, but no measurable information on other aspects of life.

Team Communication

Request that your allies work together. They might not start as a team, particularly if there are cultural or mythic differences among them. They need to communicate together to effectively help you. Most move in harmony, working out their differences and opinions beyond our perception of space and time. When we communicate with them, they already know their group message. A small core forms, working together to fulfill the roles needed in a good team. One spirit ally takes the leading role and is in frequent contact. Other allies come and go as you need them. Some are always present, but when their talents are not needed, they fade into the background. After a time of no contact, you start to forget them. Have no fear, spirits do not hold grudges as people do. Honor them and your experiences with them, but if they slip your mind, there is a reason. I write down all my experiences with spirits and periodically review them. Like looking at a journal, reflecting on the year, I review the experiences with my allies. This way I honor our time together and value the spirit, even if we are no longer working together.

Blind Obedience

People who actively work with spirit allies in all forms most often stress that they are allies, no matter what you call them. They are friends, helpers, and guides, but equals. The relationship is like having a spiritual big brother or sister, or even aunt or uncle. Though you often follow their instructions, you are not meant to follow messages blindly, even when they come for our highest good. Allies offer help and work in partnership and cooperation with you. Ask questions for a better understanding.

Even when working with Great Spirit, or any other direct incarnation of the divine, like the gods and goddess from across the world, you do not have to follow blindly. Most of these beings come in unconditional love, and while they need to be respected, like all allies, they do not order.

Do not get into a submissive role with your allies because they do not want your blind obedience. Only harmful spirits want that. No growth comes from blind obedience. Strong allies work for the highest good. They want you to live in love and happiness, doing what you need to do for your own transformation.

◎ MY SUPPORT TEAM ◎

My own support team has been varied over the years. I was raised Catholic and believed in ghosts. I had the experience in high school with the spirit of my great aunt. The ideas behind the spirit world made sense to me. I believed in something, but I was not sure what it was.

I was introduced to my first guides while studying witchcraft rather early in life. I learned that witchcraft encourages the responsibility of the individual in thought and deed. Nothing is blamed on a devil. Witches do not even believe in a devil. They work with natural energy and honor the cycles of Earth and the stars. They heal, do magic, and work with spirits.

When I was introduced to my spirit guides in a basic witchcraft class I was not sure if they were real. The whole time I wondered if I had made up the experience. I do have an active imagination and love to read science fiction and fantasy books. The reading material for the class was heavy in popular psychology along with the occult, so I took the view that spirit guides could be my own mind giving me counsel or the anima/animus theory.

Many years later I found the meditative technique my witchcraft teacher used was very similar to the Silva Method. In your mind's eye you create a laboratory or inner workshop, a place of personal power. From there two guides meet you, one masculine and one feminine, to counsel you in any work you do.

My first guide was a woman. She looked like an Arabian princess with golden dark skin and pink veils. Her eyes were beautiful and she had pointed ears like an elf. I never had any previous connection to Arabia or the Middle East in general, so I thought the image of her rather weird. My male guide looked a lot like an acquaintance I knew in passing. I also knew this tall, lanky, blond man in real life to be a witch. I thought I had associated his image with my male magical self because I did not know any other male witches. That could still be true. My teacher implied this person's higher self could be my guide.

A basic visual was as far as I got with the meditation. I saw my guides' lips move, but could never hear what they were saying. The experience did not weigh heavily on my mind, since at the time I was not interested in spirit guides. I wanted to learn magic.

A few months later, with some practice, I began to hear my guides clearly and learned their names were Asha and Llan. Their advice was hard to hear since I had not worked on opening my psychic senses. I still chalked it up to either my imagination or my own mind giving me advice. I did not even understand the concept of spirit guides, and information was not readily available. My eyes opened a little wider when I learned of a friend's experience years earlier in the same course. Her female guide gave her the name of a relatively obscure Celtic heroine or goddess. My friend knew nothing of Celtic mythology, so I knew she was not making it up or remembering something she read.

Even further down the road, in a spiritual discussion group online, I found a woman who worked with a female spirit guide named Asha. I asked my Asha if this was true. She told me that she would be bored if she had to always wait for me to talk to her, and then laughed. After that, I started consulting her more. Asha has helped me with my own emotional work, learning to heal myself and heal others.

Llan is more into information and teaching. If I have a question, I go to him since he probably has the answer or will tell me where to go to get it. Even though he seems like Mr. Spock from *Star Trek*, being very logical, he is now showing me a softer side and looking at the instinctual and emotional components of learning.

Soon after speaking with them both, I had many dreams of a third guide, an older woman named Myrtle. She works with me during my dreams, taking me to libraries and classrooms, or on cosmic field trips. Sometimes I would awaken with images of myself and a few other people sitting around a table, painting geometric patterns in the air with our minds. Each image packed a lot of information, but I was uncertain of the meanings. I know I do not have to know. I am learn-ing what I need on that level, and it will filter down to the conscious level when I need it. I get the feeling Myrtle really is not a little old lady with big glasses and curlers. She wears a shroud my subcon-scious gives her. Very rarely have I spoken to her consciously, since she shows up in only my deepest meditations.

Macha is part of the Celtic triple goddess, as the crone or mother aspect. She tells me she has been all three before, maiden, mother, and crone, and will be all three again. I was first introduced to her in ritual magic. Positioned in the South with the element of air, my tradition called on the Crow and the Crow Mother Macha. She is associated with the horse and the underworld as well. Some of her stories are fierce, filled with curses. Severed heads on the battlefield were called Macha's acorns. When we called her name, I felt a strong presence. Even indoors you could feel a breeze blow. I called on her more and more, feeling she was my patron. You learn many shamanic techniques in witchcraft, and while journeying in the shamanic otherworlds in a trance, I started to see crows. Then I would see many crows in the physical world. Crows became one of my power animals.

Then in my meditations Macha visited me. She is my guardian and guide, and in a lot of ways, the ally and friend I value most. She brings a feeling of safety, but has encouraged my life changes in stun-ningly positive ways. She encouraged my education into other eso-teric arts and holistic healing and she told me to teach and write. When I take workshops, I feel her behind me, her great wings out-stretched. Before I related any of this information, a psychic told me he saw someone with iridescent black wings all around me. Macha guides my every step and is now here, even as I write this.

Macha, Asha, and Llan have become the core of my own spiritual support team. Since then, I have attracted a number of spirits. Some are still with me. Others have left. Sometimes they give me names only to be used between us. A prominent figure right now is Spider Grandmotherfather. I have done a lot of journey work with the Spider totem. I have found totems in the dolphin, one in particular named Shasha, and the winged feathered serpent, the Coatl, from Aztec myth.

I commune with Gaia, the Earth goddess consciousness of our planet, almost daily. She has a wonderful voice. The goddess Kali from Hindu myths and the horned god Cernunnos from the Celtic tradition work with me. My own magical style is drawing on many cultures and deities. Kali seems to be shadowing many of my coven members, since we are all going through great changes. Erzulie, Dionysus, Pele, Pan, and Tlazoteotl are other goddess and gods who have visited me. In ritual I have called upon Cerridwen, Odin, Lugh, Bel, Danu, Dagda, Isis, and Osiris. Although I do not usually speak with them as I would other spirit allies, I definitely feel their presence with me in a ritual circle.

I do work with my higher self and my shadow self. They make a lovely pair. I continue to heal my disassociation from angels. My coven's rituals call on the archangels Michael, Uriel, Gabriel, and Raphael with success, along with the archangel Metatron. My own guardian angel is named Arak, who seems nice enough but is not particularly chatty. As the lightworker's paradigm sneaks into my personal cosmology, I find myself connecting with Pleiadian Archangels, medical teams from the Great White Brotherhood and Ascended Masters like Quan Yin and one whom I originally knew only as the "Man Who Changes." Since then he revealed one of his past lives as the Celtic hero and magician Gwydion. The overlap between two so seemingly different groups is wonderful to see. There is so much more in common among most spiritual practices than you would think as long as they are entered with the highest intent.

As my experiences change, my beliefs about them shift as well. I am no longer coming from the place where I think this is my imagination. As I list some of my allies, I realize it is a pretty big circle of friends. Some work with the core team. Others just stay to themselves. I think my spirit allies have a separate and distinct consciousness, but the more I study metaphysics, the harder it is to explain *separate* and *distinct*. We are all connected. We are all part of the divine mind. We are all part of the one spirit running through all life, physical and spiritual. How can we be separate? But I think they are as distinct as you and I and every other person around us. They are individuals. They have their own lessons and experiences.

I think there is a world of possibilities out there for the support team, and I spend a lot of time exploring and questioning them. Your own support team can be diverse and colorful or simply one trusted guide filling many roles. Honor your own truths and experiences. Some allies leave me questioning and reevaluating my entire belief system, which is good. Anyone, spirit or otherwise, who encourages you to think for yourself, should be welcomed into your life.

CHAPTER FIVE

LEARNING TO PLAY

IF WE ARE STILL PRETENDING to be secret agents deep under cover, like good old James Bond, then you must be feeling like you have lost your secret communicator watch and decoder ring. If this whole support team is here for you, to aid you in all your plans with protection, information, advice, and power, how do you access them? You need to tune in to the right frequency.

◎ OUR INTERNAL TECHNOLOGY ◎

Our most important technology is internal. We do not need an alarm clock to wake up at seven A.M. Before you go to bed simply tell your internal clock to wake at the right time. Visualize yourself waking then or visualize the clock. This strategy does not always work at first, so set your mechanical alarm for ten minutes past your internal clock alarm. Eventually your body gets in synch.

Internal clocks are one form of inner technology, but there are many others. A doctor is not needed to tell us we are sick. We know, but choose not to listen. As our body knows how to get sick, it knows how to reverse the process. Medicine helps us in our own healing process, but no one heals us but ourselves. Sweaters are unnecessary in the cold. We can tell our bodies to adjust to the change in temperature. A polygraph is not needed to tell us someone is lying. We know that, too, if we block out the ego and listen to the gut. When we give our power away to an external device, we forget it and we lose that power. To work with spirit allies, you have to recover your lost internal technology–your psychic abilities.

Psychic abilities are not powers beyond the scope of ordinary mortals. Everyone has them–we have only forgotten. Psychics are not superhuman. Think of psychic powers as a language. Everybody learns to read, write, and speak the native language. The ability is a skill to learn, but everyone has the potential. Most people learn language easily because they are taught as children and are constantly exposed to it. People in modern societies, for the most part, lack the psychic languages because they are never taught or encouraged when growing up. Now these languages must be rediscovered.

Psychic powers are like languages. We all have the potential to learn them. The ability depends on our exposure, practice, and raw talent. Most people can write a note, but very few can write a novel. Everyone is psychic, but not everyone can tell exactly what I am thinking at a given moment. There are levels of skill, but the psychic ability necessary to contact our allies is comparable to writ- ing a letter or picking up the phone. Most everyone can do that. Different techniques exist, so if you have difficulty with one, you can try another until the right one presents itself.

Two paths of psychic techniques are before you, depending on the type of information you receive. The first type is direct informa- tion. Answers to your questions are clear and precise, in a strict *yes* or *no* format. Techniques include dowsing with a pendulum, applied kinesiology, and speaking directly with your allies. The second path is symbolic information. The message is encoded in symbols and sto- ries, which you later have to interpret and decide what the message is. Shamanic journeys, visions, prophetic dreams, and tools like tarot cards fall in this category. Even if you desire to follow one path, you can find your talent in another. A few techniques cross both paths, depending on the spirit allies. You may see and hear your guide crys- tal clear, but the message given still needs to be decoded through symbolism. Automatic handwriting is a good talent to start with, since it is both direct and symbolic, depending on the user.

◎ STATE OF MIND ◎

The basic key to psychic ability is altering your state of mind. By relaxing the mind and body, you allow yourself to find the talents and abilities you need. A lot of our meditation and relaxation techniques, like prayer, chanting, and shamanic trance, do the same thing. They lower our brain waves. As we live out our lives in a fast-paced world, our brain is fairly active, dealing with direct stimulation from the world around us. We must be alert, make decisions, and cope with the outside world. Consider our modern workday as Paleolithic hunting time. We must be alert or our prey will have us for supper instead. Now, we only have to worry about coworkers and family members taking us by surprise. Our danger level is not the same.

When our brain waves are recorded in this alert state, they measure at twelve to sixteen hertz, or cycles per second, in general. Not all parts of the brain will be in this range. Some will be higher and others lower, but the average measurement will be between twelve and sixteen. This level of activity is called beta level.

The Alpha State

When our ancestors went back to the cave, or when we go back home, relax, and unwind, our brain waves decrease. If we meditate or use specific relaxation techniques like music, chanting, stretching, or visualization, brain waves go lower still. The level below beta is called alpha, measuring eight to twelve hertz. We are relaxed, but still aware. The relaxed state of being opens our inner world. Alpha opens the doors to our internal technology. Psychic talents are hiding within us.

Alpha is all that is necessary for psychic experiences. Some people are very surprised to find out how simple it is. Think of a daydream–the wispy feeling you have when you think of nothing and let the mind wander. That feeling is alpha. No bells or whistles go off when you are in alpha. You experience alpha during sleep, before reaching deeper states. You hit it several times in the day as your mind wanders. If you can daydream, you can have a psychic experience.

When you reach this state, your ego takes a backseat. With your conscious mind out of the way, you open to channel information purely. *Pure* is a relative term. Even the most talented psychic will admit to sometimes tainting information because of his own hopes and fears. The ego is filtering the message. Our goal is to relax the ego. Thank it for sharing and then tell it to go in another room and relax. Once you detach yourself from the outcome, you have more accurate results. If you want to hear a *yes* and someone is trying to tell you *no,* you will still hear a *yes* if you let the ego get in the way. That is why it is important to relax and let go of your concerns. Any stable meditation or spiritual practice that quiets the mind helps you cultivate this temporary state of detachment. Many Eastern traditions try to cultivate a state of detachment throughout life, but westerners usually find this a difficult goal. If you are completely detached and at peace all the time, you probably do not need the direct help of your spirit allies, but you can still enjoy your experiences with them. This time becomes more play than guidance.

Some psychics enter deeper trance states. Spiritual practices around the world usually encourage the deeper state of relaxation and union. Their techniques lead to the theta and delta levels below alpha. Some psychic experiences occur in the higher ranges above beta, roving into the areas called high beta, k complex, and super-high beta. Intense out-of-body and kundalini experiences are particularly marked by these higher ranges.

Psychic phenomena are not limited to alpha, but learning alpha to enter a receptive meditative state is an easy way to start the process. Now you have the key. Simply open the door.

A Relaxation Exercise

Here is a simple relaxation exercise using breath, sensation, and visualization. When visualizing, picture a screen in your mind's eye. Imagine you are watching a movie or slide show. Let the colors and descriptions wash over you. Do not try to get them perfect. If you get agitated about not doing them perfectly, they are hindering you. They are only to help you lower your brain waves. If you see a flash of the color or get a simple impression with no visual, it is all right. You are doing fine. That is a common experience. Go with the flow. Visualizing the colors helps relax and balance you and your energy centers in the body, the chakras. Most focus on seven chakras, but there are chakras between these seven, making twelve main energy centers along the spine. These twelve colors help us reconnect with the chakras and our inner abilities. It can help to tape these exercise or have a friend read them to you.

EXERCISE 1 – ALTERING CONSCIOUSNESS

❶ Take deep, relaxing breaths in and out. Release all that does not serve your highest good. Do not force or strain. Let the breath flow naturally. Relax. With each breath out, all tension and unwanted thoughts flow out.

❷ Imagine a bell or a gong above your head. When this bell is struck, the most relaxing sound comes out from it. The waves of sound flow through your body, starting at the head, through the trunk, down the arms and legs, to the feet. Each wave of relaxation neutralizes all tension and stress. You relax your body completely. Strike the bell as many times as needed, and let the relaxing sounds flow.

❸ Tell yourself to relax your body, mind, and spirit. You are in your meditative state.

❹ Visualize the screen of your mind. On it imagine a splash of color, starting from red and moving through the spectrum. T of each item to help you with the color. With each color, count backward from 12 to 1 You can visualize the numbers drawn in those colors or on a colored background, but do not force the experience if the visualization is difficult for you.

> 12—RED, red like an apple
> 11—RED-ORANGE, like the glowing embers of a fire
> 10—ORANGE, like the fruit
> 9—GOLD, like the metal in a ring
> 8—YELLOW, like a lemon
> 7—GREEN, like grass
> 6—AQUA, like ocean water
> 5—BLUE, like the sky
> 4—INDIGO, like the night sky
> 3—PURPLE, like a grape
> 2—VIOLET, like violet flowers
> 1—CRYSTAL WHITE, like a quartz crystal or prism

⑤ You are now at your alpha state. Everything you do here is for your highest good, harming none. You are open only to guides and allies who come for your highest good. Count backward from 13 to 1 if you feel you need to go deeper.

This exercise can be done anytime before trying a psychic or divination technique to contact your spirit allies. Many of the exercises in this book use this exercise as their first step. With a little practice and body memory, you can probably stop around Step 3 to achieve a light meditative state and reserve the color countdown for when a deeper state is needed.

If the color countdown is difficult, substitute imagery more suited to you. A popular technique is to imagine counting backward down a flight of stairs. The stairs are numbered and painted the different colors. Each stair might light up with the color when stepped on. Someone once told me she imagines stairs, but the colors were like walking through a sunset or colored mist. Modify Exercise 1 as needed.

To return, count from 1 to 12 without colors after any of these meditations and exercises.

◎ DIVINATION ◎

Divination means "to divine," for the very act of getting information from our psychic senses is divine. It is part of our own god/goddess spiritual nature. Divination is a gift from the creator. Through a nonlinear process of opening your psychic skills, you divine information, usually about the future. When working in the future you are walking through the world of possibilities, of what might be. You are like Scrooge from *A Christmas Carol*. You can see the future and have the power to change it. Divination is not restricted to the future. Any kind of information is given. You can learn about the past or the present. The skills of divination are useful when contacting your spirit allies.

There are as many systems of divination as there are diviners. The process works through symbolism, so tarot cards and runes are popular. You can look for symbols in a cup of tea leaves, in wax in water, or in a crystal ball, but when working with allies for direct guidance, its best to have a direct method. You need something telling you *yes* or *no* in answer to the questions asked. One of the best tools is the pendulum.

The Pendulum

A pendulum is simply a length of cord with a weight on the end. It can be as elaborate as a crystal point on the end of a silver chain or as simple as a piece of string with a steel nut tied to the end. You hold the end of the cord and let the weight dangle. The response comes from the way the weight moves on the string. Your allies subtly influence the tool to give you the correct response. The pendulum measures energy and can be used with healing work, measuring the chakra energy centers. With allies, it is measuring the energy of their response.

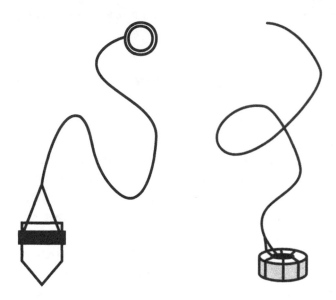

Figure 2. Pendulums

Elaborate systems have been created indicating what each move-ment means. Traditionally, clockwise is a positive or *yes* response. Counterclockwise is *no*. Swinging back and forth is *maybe* or *unsure*. I use this system myself, but it is best to find the correct indications for you. For you, a positive answer could be swinging back to front and a negative one swinging side to side. Later the pendulum can be put over a sheet of paper with many choices and the pendulum will swing toward the most appropriate one. Start with simple *yes* and *no* questions because they are the easiest. Get a pendulum or make one and try this exercise.

EXERCISE 2 – PENDULUM QUESTIONS

❶ First, you must clear the pendulum of any other vibrations that can influence it. Hold it in your hands and say, "In the name of the God/Goddess/Great Spirit [or whatever divine power you use], cleanse and neutralize this pendulum of all harmful and unwanted energy that could interfere with this reading." Inhale and blow over the pendulum. Imagine the breath a violet color, dissolving all harmful energy.

❷ Hold the pendulum in whichever hand feels comfortable, letting the weight dangle. Stop the weight from swinging so it starts in a "neutral" position.

❸ Say, "I call upon my spirit allies, only those who come for my highest good, in perfect love and trust." Ask for the best possible *yes* response for you. Wait. The pendulum will swing in a manner that indicates *yes* for you. When the answer is clear, ask for the best possible negative, or *no* response for you. The pendulum will shift. Wait until the response is clear to you. Relax and try not to think about it—just let it happen. If it is not clear, tell your allies you need a clearer response. Then ask again.

❹ Start asking simple questions that have no emotional charge for you. Ask, "Is my name _____ ?" Fill in your name and see if you get a *yes*. Or fill in someone else's name and wait for a *no*. Ask questions about the name, address, age, or height of a family member.

❺ Once you feel confident, start asking questions to which you do not know the answers. Remember to always phrase it as a *yes* or *no* question. Ask if a friend is home now. Right after the pendulum session, call your friend and find out.

❻ Now ask a question for which you need guidance. Form it as a *yes* or *no* question. If looking for a new job, take each prospective employer and ask, "Is it in my highest good to apply for this position?" Do not ask "Will I get this job if I apply for it" because sometimes going on an interview will lead to something better than the job advertised. Be careful how you phrase things, and always ask if it is for your highest good. You will find ways to adapt this technique to suit you.

At first you will feel as if you are moving the string: I want a *yes* so I am moving it clockwise. One of my students says she closes her eyes and thinks of something peaceful and soothing, like a scenic forest view. With a relaxing visual, she is not visualizing the pendulum going the way she wants it to go. This woman is very psychic and fears her abilities will telekinetically influence the outcome. Since she is physical, she could have a stronger influence over the physical world than some of her allies. If you feel you are not getting an accurate response, start again by cleansing the pendulum, or try at another time. Your daily mind-set can influence it. Most people do not need to get into a deeper meditative state for pendulum use. The invocation to the allies is enough. If you are having difficulties, do Exercise 1 to get yourself into a more receptive state. Remember, pendulum use is very accurate, but it is not foolproof. Like any psychic tool, we have the ability to block its use.

Muscle Testing

Another method of divining *yes* or *no* answers from guides is applied kinesiology, also called muscle testing. Our body is an electrical system. It has inherent body wisdom in it. Our guides can put a negative or positive response into the electrical system. A negative response weakens the system, while a positive response keeps it strong. We create a circuit with our fingers, and if that circuit breaks, the response is negative; if it holds, our answer is positive.

I learned the most popular technique for muscle testing from Machaelle Small Wright's Perelandra books, but I later found it is used by many practitioners. This method is easy because it requires only one person. Some other techniques require another person pushing down on your arm or other parts of your body.

To use the one-person method, take your receptive, less dominant hand, usually the left, and form a ring with your pinky and your thumb. This is your circuit. Take the index finger and thumb of your projective, or dominant hand–the hand with which you write–make a point, and put the point in the ring made by your receptive hand. Ask your question. Now without thinking about it, use all your strength to keep the receptive hand's ring together, while using all your projective hand's strength to open your fingers wide, to break the ring.

If your pinky and thumb come apart easily, then the answer is *no*. If they stay together, the answer is *yes*. Do not struggle or try to tire your hands. The answer comes in the first second or two. Try it. You will be surprised how immediate the response it. Follow the instructions for Exercise 2. Instead of using the pendulum, ask the same questions using the muscle-testing technique. Still invoke your spirit allies and ask for the answer to be for the highest good. You do not have to cleanse as for the pendulum, but ask "that I be a clear channel for this information from my spirit allies."

Ask for help in discerning your responses if you feel you are making them up. They will probably clear up quickly. Try Exercise 1 to get into a meditative state. One technique could suit you while the other does not. Personally, I like the muscle testing because it does not require a tool. You can ask anywhere. However, I find the pendulum to be slightly more accurate for me.

Automatic Writing

The last divination technique discussed here is the art of automatic handwriting–also called spirit writing. This skill is more complicated than the simple *yes* or *no* format, but the information given is much more personal and detailed.

Just as muscle testing puts a response into the body, automatic writing puts information directly into the body system, releasing it through writing. For those who cannot hear their allies, this lets their information and personality come through. Many people who start with automatic writing follow with other psychic experiences and then drop the technique all together in favor of more direct communication. Automatic writing bypasses the conscious mind. You have to then read what you wrote to consciously know the message. Think of it as opening the door past the veil even wider.

When you put pen to paper, do not think about anything. Just let the arm flow. Ask your questions out loud and let the body respond first. Your writing might be messy, but this is really your allies' writing. If you work with several different spirits, you can see the different styles of handwriting that come out, along with different uses of grammar and syntax. You might find yourself writing in languages you do not consciously know and need them translated. If this happens, ask the guide to communicate in English. Those beyond the veil are not bound by language.

During my automatic writing sessions, I now feel more like someone is dictating to me. I try to write down the message with no editing. Automatic writing works for guides, but most power animals will not respond using this method. Any spirit that would not normally communicate with writing or language, especially if it has never had a humanoid life, will not always respond to this method.

Start with a good supply of paper and pens. You never know how long the sessions will last. I like loose sheets of paper. That way you can just throw them out of your way. Number the pile first, to keep track of the order. Fiddling with notebooks interrupts the spontaneous flow you create. Get a good ink pen that writes quickly and does not stick. Pencils or crayons are better for some.

Never erase or fix anything until you have finished your session. Later you can go back and edit. Prevent your conscious mind from getting involved until afterward. If possible, list the questions you want to ask beforehand, or have a partner read them so you do not have to think about them. A partner can guide the session if you fear getting in too deep. Once you have some experience, you can guide a session by yourself, but first, if possible, try this exercise with a friend.

EXERCISE 3 – AUTOMATIC WRITING

❶ First, make a short list of questions you want to ask. Start with general questions, then get into more specific topics in your

life. Keep the list under ten questions. Some of your first questions may be "Who are you?" and "Where are you from?"

❷ Have your partner guide you through Exercise 1 to enter a
receptive state. Make sure your pens and paper are in front of
you.

❸ Invoke your spirit allies by saying, "I call upon my spirit allies,
only those who come for my highest good, in perfect love and
trust. I call on only those who come for the highest good and
no others." The person doing the writing should say this, but
the partner can guide him through it.

❹ Wait a few moments and allow your ally to come in and set up
a link with you. Then start asking your questions. It is best to
read them out loud at first. The partner can read them first,
then the writer can repeat them. Once the question is asked,
put pen to paper and let the body move.

❺ Read the answers only when you are finished writing. Your partner can read them to you so as to not break your mood. The
answers given usually provoke new questions. Continue as long
as you feel comfortable and psychically up to it.

⑥ Thank your spirit allies and say good-bye to them.

As with the pendulum, you may feel like you are making up the
answers you want. Close your eyes or look away. This can help
occupy your conscious mind. On the other hand, you could be
shocked at the answers you get, giving you information you had no
conscious knowledge of. Let it flow. Do not judge until after the
session. Then, with your rational aspect, discern if this is the truth,
or if this particular truth applies to you. Do not be frightened by
powerful, life-changing statements, as long as they come in perfect
love and truth. If you ask such a question in the first place, you are
ready for a life-changing answer. Automatic writing is the fir
to changing your worldview by allowing new information t

into your consciousness. Such writing opens the doors to your own transformation.

If at anytime you feel uncomfortable with the beings you are contacting, stop. This is fairly rare, particularly with the invocation in Step 3, but if they ever threaten you or give messages coming from a place of ego, either their own ego or yours, they do not come in love. If they tell you that you and only you are special and above everyone else, they do not come for your highest good. Repeat the invocation three times. Ask them to leave three times, in the name of the divine power you work with. Call upon your guardian spirits or just stop doing the writing. For some spirits not on the highest planes, this is a game akin to Ouija board. They wish to be taken seriously while they play with you. If you ignore them, they go away. If their presence or energy persists, use a clearing substance, like sage or rose water, to purify the space and trans-mute lower energies.

If you are a child of the modern world and feel more comfort-able using a keyboard than writing, computers are an excellent medium for this kind of work. The emphasis is on what you are most comfortable with and ultimately what is more effective.

◎ ORACLES AND SCRYING ◎

Feel free to explore other divination methods when connecting with your spirit allies. The pendulum, muscle testing, and automatic writing are good to start with because each requires no previous information or training. Other systems need a greater understand-ing of symbols and methods of reading them. Tarot cards, runes, and I Ching are popular oracles used to gain guidance. Many of these methods are called "throwing the bones" because some people use small animal bones or stones with pictures. The items are chosen and thrown out over an area, or in the case of tarot cards, laid out in a spread. The different formations among the symbols, where they are, and what they are next to, determine the meanings. Intuitively, the reader interprets the symbols to answer questions and gain information. Some methods can answer simple *yes* or *no* questions. If more positive, beneficial symbols are chosen, the answer is *yes*. If more negative or detrimental symbols are chosen, the answer is *no*. These systems give more detailed information, depending on how skilled the reader is.

Another intuitive way of getting information is the art of scrying, or magical seeing. Scrying is looking into a medium both with your physical and psychic eyes, letting images and symbols form in answer to your questions. The images are interpreted to fit the situation. Scrying is much more free form, since there is no standard set of symbols, as found in a deck of cards or set of stones. The images are more personal and subjective to the reader, like in a dream. The most famous scrying tool is the crystal ball. It need not be a sphere; any transparent crystal will do. Some prefer clear crystal. I like those with fractures.

Crystals are not the only medium. Some people gaze into glasses of water, tranquil pools and puddles, black or silver mirrors, clouds in the sky, tea leaves, or melted wax in water. The shapes answer your questions. You can see a Y for *yes* and an N for *no*. Images of dollar signs, coins, or crowns spark an answer of finances and money. Rings indicate a marriage. Animal shapes bring other answers, depending on what that animal means to you.

If you are familiar with these practices or want to experiment with them, they can all be combined into your spirit ally work. Usually when doing divination like this, we are connecting to our own greater knowing, slipping out of our normal view of space and time, to gain a greater perspective. In this case, start with and speak an intention that clearly states you want to connect and communicate to your spirit allies through this oracle. The images provided or the symbols chosen and the interpretation will reflect what the allies are communicating to you. Ask them to speak through the oracle device.

◎ PSYCHIC SENSES ◎

Now with some divination under your belt, you can experiment with widening your psychic senses. Divination is fueled by psychic ability, giving us tools to focus the natural power. The tools and techniques have a certain time-honored power to them already, and we are tapping in to the phenomenon. They help those who are not confident about their own inner technology. Once you see how they work, it is a small step to start using these powers directly.

Clairaudience

Clairaudience is one of the most useful psychic skills when working with our spirit friends. Imagine you are a living radio receiver, because you are. You do not pick up AM/FM, but you can receive transmissions from spirits. They come through other intermediaries, like our allies, but they all travel on the spiritual frequency. Opening your clairaudient powers is like turning on the radio and tuning in to the right frequency. We each have our own broadcast wavelength. That way, you get only the messages for you, and I get the messages for me. Some talented psychics can change their frequency and tune in to their client's guides, giving them messages directly. I find it more empowering to help another find her guidance by working in her current belief system. People can believe in their spirits allies or just in a strengthening of their own inner voice and intuition.

With clairaudience, you hear the message. It is a different experience for everyone. Some physically feel the words, as they would in the ears, coming in from the outside. The process has a definite physical vibration to it. When it comes in this strongly, budding psychics think they are going mad, hearing voices. More commonly, people feel it right above the ears, near the temples, or directly in the brain as if someone were talking through their crown. I usually do not physically feel it. The communication is an internal voice, like my conscience. At first words start popping into my mind, but I know I am not thinking them. They are mostly in my own internal voice. Little by little each spirit's personality comes through. Later I can tell immediately by the tone, inflection, and words who was speaking. I still discern to make sure it was a spirit I know.

Clairaudience is the basic skill used in channeling. Channeling is a lot like automatic writing. It is a way to get information out directly with the interface of spirit and body. A couple of methods of channeling exist, including conscious channeling, full-body channeling, and a mixture of the two. I suggest trying these methods only when you have some more experience with spirits in general and feel confident about your allies, limits, and abilities.

The following exercise can build up your psychic ears. Etheric muscles and skills need to be exercised like any other. You will need something that makes a tone, something soothing and meditative like a bell, chime, gong, or Tibetan singing bowl. A few glasses filled with different levels of water will do. Or you can sit in front of a piano. Use something that will play one semisustained note without requiring too much effort on your part.

EXERCISE 4 – DEVELOPING PSYCHIC HEARING

❶ Do Exercise 1 to enter a receptive state. Make sure your musical tools are in easy reach.

❷ Close your eyes and play one note. Strike your bell, gong, or other instrument. Listen closely.

❸ When the sound fades, silence the instrument so no note is being made, no vibration.

❹ Remember the simple sound. Hear it in your head. Let it flow without worrying about it.

❺ Try this exercise with different notes or instruments. Try to imagine in your mind the timbre, pitch, color, and quality of the sound. The more you practice, the more details you will hear and remember. Try it again, listening more carefully to the sound.

⑥ Then try the exercise with music. Excerpts from slow instrumental pieces are best so you will not focus on the words. Listen for only thirty to sixty seconds. Then replay the music in your head. Focus on the melody at first, but then work your way into hearing the layers of sound behind it. This builds psychic hearing.

Clairvoyance

Clairvoyance is the next psychic sense. As our ears have a psychic counterpart, so do our eyes. Clairvoyance is psychic seeing, or seeing with the inner eye, also called the third eye or brow chakra. Anything visualized or imagined uses the inner eye. When you saw the colors in Exercise 1, you were using your inner eye. Clairvoyance

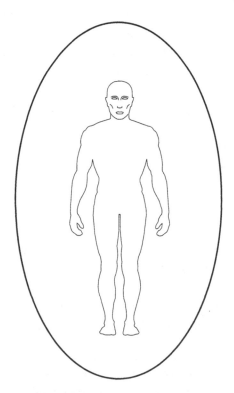

Figure 3. The Aura

allows the images to come to us, instead of our conscious mind creating them.

Our third eye lets us see energy, if we are open to it. For most people this is a foreign concept, but once you let go of your prejudices and self-imposed limitations, you will open to this talent. Psychics with this ability see energy in the body, noting sickness or health, and in the area around the body, or aura. The aura is our energy field extending out three to five feet, surrounding us like an egg or a sphere. And the third eye sees spirits. We perceive them around us in the physical world or in our own inner realms. Spirits have an energy field like an aura that can be perceived the same way. Sometimes it is subtler because there is no body to use as a focus. We never know where spirits might appear, but they are present.

The power of visualization is a key to opening the third eye. Use this exercise to strengthen your skills. You will need a white candle and a small handheld object pleasing to the eye, like a crystal or ring.

EXERCISE 5 – DEVELOPING PSYCHIC VISION

❶ Darken the room's lights and light your candle. Sit a few feet away from it, where you can comfortably stare at it.

❷ Do Exercise 1 to enter a receptive state. Make sure your object is in easy reach.

❸ Open your eyes and stare at the candle for a few moments. Try to look past it, not directly into the flame, so you do not tire your eyes. Then close your eyes and visualize the flame in your mind's eye. Do it without strain. Let the image flow naturally.

❹ When you lose the image in your mind's eye, repeat Step 3. You can do it as many times as you would like.

⑤ Open your eyes and hold the object. Look at it carefully, from any angle. Look at it until you think you see most of the details. Then close your eyes and visualize it in your mind's eye.

⑥ In your mind's eye, turn the object around, making it three-dimensional. Look at the image from every angle. Repeat Step 5 as many times as you like.

Do not expect perfect results the first time out. Like any skill, it takes practice, but some people have a knack for it. This exercise helps open your third eye. Try it with different objects until you feel fairly confident in your abilities. Then just imagine things with-out physically seeing them. See them only in your mind's eye. With television and computers, our imaginations often atrophy a bit, and we need simple experiences to jump-start them.

Clairsentience

The last psychic skill we are working with is clairsentience, or psy-chic knowing—without the use of auditory messages or visuals, we just know something. A friend calls this "the knowing" and feels it is one of the most important skills available. You do not know how or why, you simple sense things. Something is certain in your mind, but you have no logical reason for it. People are much more famil-iar with clairsentience as intuition or a gut feeling. I am sure every-body reading this book has had an experience of knowing some-thing for no rational reason.

Some allies work through this sense simply by letting you know things or encouraging your own intuition. Some people feel spirits as physical sensations. When working with a spirit, you can feel its presence, its vibe, which comes across as a feeling of cold or warmth. You sense the air around it somehow shift. You feel the spirit's energy directly, or feel it in your body if it touches you. These are all forms of clairsentience, a powerful experience.

To open this power, and in fact all psychic power, you must open your heart. The heart chakra is truly the gateway to our per-

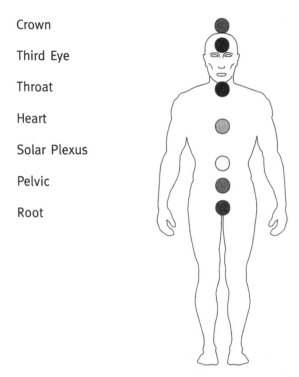

Crown

Third Eye

Throat

Heart

Solar Plexus

Pelvic

Root

Figure 4. The Seven Main Chakras

sonal power. If we cannot use our gifts with love and compassion, we will not access them. That is not to say some have not learned to work psychic skill without the heart, but there are always reper-cussions to such power without love. To start your own inner jour-ney, ask to open your heart.

The next exercise opens your chakras, grounding you and cen-tering you in love. The meditation opens the heart for love; the throat, which control clairaudience; the third eye for clairvoyance; and the crown for clairsentience, our divine knowing. These are four of the seven major chakras. The other three are the solar plexus below the ribs, concerned with energy and power; the pelvic chakra for instinct and trust; and the root chakra for survival. All seven are balanced with this exercise.

EXERCISE 6 – OPENING THE CHAKRAS

1 Do Exercise 1 to enter a meditative state.

2 Say, "I ask to be connected to the love and light of the God/Goddess/Great Spirit [or whatever divine power you use]." Visualize a ball of white light above your head. The light is pure and full of love.

3 The ball of light descends down into your crown, opening the space atop your skull. Each chakra is a wheel of light. As the ball passes through it, the wheel spins faster. All blocks are cleared and the crown chakra opens.

4 The ball of light quickly descends in a line parallel to your spine, going all the way through your trunk. It opens and clears your seven major chakras, the crown, third eye, throat, heart, solar plexus, pelvic, and root. When it reaches your root, it continues to descend, creating a line of light into the center of Earth. You are grounded to Earth.

5 The ball of light rises back up the grounding line and through your body, stopping at the heart. Your heart opens to the powers of love and compassion.

6 The ball rises to your throat. Your throat chakra opens you to the powers of both psychic hearing and speaking. This is the power of communication.

7 The ball rises to your third eye chakra, which opens to the powers of psychic seeing.

8 The ball rises to your crown. Now thank your divinity for these gifts. The ball rises above your head and disappears as it ascends.

You can do this exercise before Exercises 2 through 5. Do it daily even if you are not doing other work. It is a good habit to open the psychic powers and bring health to the body.

◎ JOURNEYING ◎

Shamanic journeying, working in the unseen realms, is our last arena, and perhaps one of the most fun. Within each of us is a natural connection to the unseen realms. You may call them the collective unconscious, the astral plane, or the other side of the veil, but they are working with the same concepts. These realms are an intermediary place between those in a body and those who are not. They are the otherworlds.

A basic concept in this type of travel is the belief in three worlds, usually connected by a world tree or mountain. Our physical world is the middle world, where time and space exist. Our thoughts still control our reality, but there is a lag time, and our visualizations do not always manifest the way we want them. Around us are the upper and lower worlds. There your thoughts can create your reality immediately, but you are also sharing the space with many other beings. You can experience the fantastic feats of myth, including flight, superstrength, and resurrection.

The upper world is a place where you meet divine beings who give you direct information and spiritual enlightenment. The lower world is primal and dreamlike, where you unravel the mysteries and follow your instincts. It brings healing and regeneration. The upper and lower worlds are found in mythology, from the Christian Heaven and Hell to the Norse Asgard and Hel. Some realms are generalized, while others are specific, magical places. The otherworlds are described as under the ocean, in the clouds, or on an island. Both kinds of worlds can be launch pads into myriad mysterious lands and adventures not found anywhere but in our personal mythos.

Allies work with you in these states. Here in the otherworlds all of your allies can make contact. Power animals are most frequent and often the first experience here, but any beings can move through these realms. Like any adventure, be careful and use your intuition. The symbolism can be confusing.

Using Sound to Enter the Otherworlds

Sound is a great aid for entering the deep shamanic state, perceiving the otherworlds. Tapes with drums or rattles can be an immense help, or a partner can drum or rattle for us. I prefer a tape if the partners have no previous drumming experience; they can always drum along with a tape when learning. Drumming music by Michael Harner, author of *Way of the Shaman,* is great for this purpose and available at many New Age shops. And I highly recommend his book for more information on modern shamanism.

Even though we are lowering our brain waves, the beat needs to be fairly fast, from roughly 140 to 200 beats a minute. Slower sounds can actually hinder us until we are in our shamanic state. Journeying can be done with other instrumental music or no sound at all. Blindfolds to block out the light can help us to focus on our inner sight.

The following short, introductory journey is to help you be aware of the three worlds. We start with the world tree, the cosmic axis linking the upper, middle, and lower worlds. Do not attempt to go further yet.

EXERCISE 7 – INTRODUCTION TO JOURNEYING

❶ Lie down on your back. Cover your eyes. Get comfortable.

❷ Do Exercise 1 to reach a meditative state. If you have a drumming tape, play it. Choose the shortest selection, from five to fifteen minutes, or have your partner guide you through Exercise 1 and start drumming if you choose to use live music.

❸ In your mind's eye, see a very large tree, with roots digging into the earth and branches rising up high in the sky. It looks bigger than any tree you have ever seen.

❹ Imagine this picture on the screen of your mind as a window. Open the window and step through. You are standing before the tree.

❺ Look for an opening near the tree. It is in the roots or trunk or next to the tree, like a hole or dark pool of water.

❻ Enter the opening and explore the tunnel. It is like the birth canal into the next world. You are ascending to the upper world or descending to the lower world.

❼ Look for a light at the end of the tunnel. Look through the light, but do not leave the tunnel.

❽ Return to where you started. Take nothing back with you. This is just an introduction to the world tree.

❾ Return your perceptions to the room. Most drumming tapes have a "call back," a break in the rhythm serving to bring your attention back to the room. From the call back you have a few moments to complete your journey.

Drink water and take it easy after the journey. First experiences with the world tree can tire people easily and cause detoxification of the body in some. If your images were not vivid, do not worry; they grow over time. Just go with the experience and perceptions you did have. Your dreams over the next few days might reveal more about your journey.

Dreams

Dreams in general are an important aspect of journey work. If you are not yet capable of consciously traversing the otherworlds, but desire to contact your allies, they can work with you through your higher self and dreams to reveal further information from previous journeys. The intent and desire to contact them is enough to start this process. I suggest you keep a dream journal by your bed at night. Write down the first thoughts and dreams in the morning. If they do not seem significant, have no fear. In a few weeks, review them and discover reoccurring themes you may have.

If you need guidance on a problem in your life and need a solution, you can use your dream time to help you solve it. Try this the next time you go to bed. Dream work is best when relaxed and uninfluenced, so refrain from watching TV, reading, eating, or writing for an hour before this exercise.

EXERCISE 8 – DREAM JOURNEYING

❶ Invoke your spirit allies by saying, "I call upon my spirit allies, only those who come for my highest good, in perfect love and trust. I call on only those who come for the highest good and no others."

❷ Write in your dream journal your question or problem, in as much detail as you feel necessary. Ask specific questions.

❸ Ask your spirit allies for aid in finding the solution. Next to the notebook, on your nightstand you can keep any sacred object that makes you feel good. Quartz crystals are good for dream work, particularly Herkimer Diamonds. A bowl of clear water can be placed under the bed to bring clear dreams. Your crystals or dream herbs, like lavender, chamomile, skullcap, and valerian, can be added to the water. Change the water once a week.

❹ When you wake up in the morning, write down everything you can remember from the night before. Then read it over and interpret how it fits your situation.

Show your question and dream to a trusted friend to get an outside view, if needed. Even though these are your dream symbols, and you must decide their ultimate meaning, it sometimes helps to have an outside eye look at them. I am not a fan of dream dictionaries because such symbols have different meanings from culture to culture and even in individual families. Aid from one who knows you well is usually better than a textbook. Only beware of their own unconscious projections and needs of you.

For quite a while I was doing a lot of spirit dream work. I would write things like "we" and "us" but have no conscious recollection of anyone else in the dream. "We" traveled around and I know I learned many things with this group, but to this day I am not sure who they were and what we did. My guides now tell me I know everything I need to know now about that topic. If I need more on the conscious level, it will eventually filter down. I believe I was traveling with my guides or soul group.

The Vision Quest

The last type of journey is called a vision quest. This can be very intense and is not to be taken on lightly. You literally go questing for a vision. Native Americans go on a vision quest to find their allies or animals. The technique usually consisted of travel to a remote place, like a mountaintop or cave, for fasting, isolation, and the absolute darkness of night. In the center of a circle of prayer knots and personal power objects, the individuals stay until having a vision. Modern revivals of this ceremony are practiced today by people from all cultures, but should not be undertaken lightly or without the guidance of others who are more experienced.

CHAPTER SIX

MEETING YOUR SPIRIT ALLIES

THE WISDOM OF YOUR FIRST ALLIES has already taken voice through automatic writing or other divination techniques. These skills are a great asset, lasting a lifetime. Eventually you will desire to deepen your experience with your allies. Your combined skills bring you face to face, so to speak.

A lucky few do not have to do anything. Allies come without being called. Either psychic skills are advanced enough before starting this quest for allies, or the universe gleefully conspires to bring the right circumstances together. Spontaneous meetings are not common, but they do happen.

A friend who used to live in Boston met his first guides on the subway train going back to his apartment. Although I never discovered new guides on the subway train, I find myself very open to them when I am riding one. The experience could be because I try to open all my senses to be aware of my safety on these rides. I open all my psychic senses too.

If you have any type of spiritual practice already, your guides can appear there. You are already in the mind-set. You see an angel in church or hear a voice when meditating. Pondering the existence of guides brings them out of the woodwork. Many people doing home practice of a spiritual discipline, like yoga, tai chi or qi gong, suddenly feel or see another presence. Their guides drew them subconsciously to these disciplines, or they have past-life associations with these cultures. Healers using any holistic modality, but particularly energy healing, get into a meditative state during a session and see strange things, like glimpses of other people in the room, a flash of a robe, a moving shadow. They feel other people are also laying on hands, helping to move the energy. These beings are either the allies of the healers, aiding them in their calling or the allies of the client.

When these spontaneous meetings occur, you cannot quite believe they are happening, or how they are happening, but the hardest part is over. Now that you have made contact, subsequent communication will be easier.

Intentional meetings are more difficult. We purposely open our psychic skill and practice divination talents. You could feel the presence of your allies before, while in a meditative state, but through your intention, you deepen the experience and cultivate a stronger relationship. Psychic senses open and provide combinations of intuitive, visual, and auditory messages. If you do not ask for the experience, you will not get it. I use ritual along with intent to strengthen my requests, but first we should talk about safety.

◎ DISCERNMENT ◎

Discernment is simply using your better judgment. Although we open our hearts to compassion, we should not believe everyone and everything at face value. We are open to other people's beliefs and advice, but when it comes to our own happiness, we have to find what is right for us. We would be foolish to follow anyone blindly, spiritually or physically. Blind obedience is the cornerstone of a cult. We must use our minds to understand the message and determine if it is right for us.

Using Heart and Mind

True discernment comes from both the heart and mind. The message should make sense, or at the very least not hurt anyone.

Sometimes messages take awhile to make sense, but if you are told to jump off a roof, you would get hurt or killed. Would someone who is giving this spiritual advice care about you and love you? The message must resonate with the heart. Messages inspiring fear do not resonate with love. The information must come from love and a desire to genuinely help.

All my teachers have taught me, from different spiritual disciplines and in different words, that the message has to resonate with you. The information must strike a chord in the heartstrings of your soul. True spiritual guidance from a helpful, loving being expands your awareness and view. The message is compassionate and expressed for the good of all. Look out for messages that incite fear, arrogance, and division. They do not come from an expanded consciousness. Such words are your warning signs on the spiritual road.

Messages can be hard to hear emotionally. They tell us things about ourselves that we do not like to hear. They request great changes in our path, opening our heart or taking responsibility for our actions in ways we have never done before. They request we "walk our talk," meaning we truly live by the words we say, but they never demand. They point the way but do not want to live our life for us. If they do, the spirit is not a true ally.

Allies have individual personalities. Some are gruff and grumble. They can appear dark and brooding or have an unusual sense of humor, but their overall message will be filled with love. Some of the dark, pagan godesses like Macha, Kali, or Persephone are frightening at first. They help with lessons of fear. In their essence, these goddesses are motherly love–the love of a mother can be tough love.

When meeting any new spirit, use your head, use your heart, and see how your body feels. Our bodies contain inherent, natural wisdom that resonates only with the truth. Each spirit has a specific vibration. You get to know the feeling of your guide soon enough, but still use the discernment techniques.

Testing Spirits

Many spiritual schools teach that even dark and harmful spirits are required to answer truthfully if you ask them the same question three times in the name of the divine power. You can call it God, Goddess, Great Spirit, Jesus, or Divine Truth, any name works. Kunaku is the Mayan's word for the Divine Creator. It works, as does Isis or Mother Mary. Ask, "In the name of the Goddess, do you come in perfect love and perfect trust, for the highest good?" Try, "In the name of our Lord Yahweh, do you speak the absolute Divine Truth?" Request a *yes* or *no* answer. Some beings say, "I do . . . not," with the *not* very soft, when they think you have stopped listening. A true ally would not mind answering in the way you request. Harmful spirits are a devious bunch.

Another great discernment method I learned from a meditation teacher is to ask beings to send you unconditional love while saying their name three times. If they cannot do it, they are probably lying about who they are. Many spirits like to pose as other beings of great power. If you have any doubt the spirit is lying to you and you do not trust it to answer truthfully no matter how you phrase the question, this test will be the true proof. Harmful spirits, for obvious reasons, do not work in love, so they cannot send it.

Getting Rid of Unwelcome Spirits

If beings do not come in love, ask them to leave by the same power three times. Send them unconditional love and light. Visualize white light in your home space. One who is not in the light will either go toward it or shun it and leave. You cannot force harmful spirits into the light, but there is no need to put up with them. You can only request they go and show them the way.

Laughing at unwelcome spirits is another good way to make them leave. They desperately want to be taken seriously. A craving for attention is the real reason they give you advice. Most want the attention, because it feeds their thoughtform or energy body. The more people pay attention to them, the stronger they get. If you laugh at them, you rob them of any energy you gave. They leave.

Any spirit who cannot enjoy a good laugh is no fun to be around anyway. Laughter is a great component for triggering love. A lot of my allies are very playful and do silly things. Some are tricksters, but they are playful tricksters, not evil. Too many people take spirituality too seriously and would think laughing guides are less spiritual. In my view, it makes them more spiritual and loving.

Serious or playful, light or dark, do the spirits come in love? Do they offer sound advice? Do you feel good and comfortable around them? If you think *no* to any of these questions, then do not work with the spirit.

◎ DEVILS AND DEMONS ◎

"The Devil made me do it." That saying always stuck with me, an image of a horrible force taking over my body and making me do strange and hideous things. But I noticed when I, or others, did things we would call "wrong," we did them of our own free will. Later we would regret them, but at the time we chose the action. The idea of the Devil appeared less likely to me.

The Law of Polarity

The belief in an almost omnipotent force of evil does not fit my worldview. I look to the natural world, where evil is a concept created by humans. I believe the universe is in polarity, and the action of opposite forces keeps energy moving in the creative cycle. Hermetic philosophers call this the Law of Polarity. If you look at only the polarity of good and evil, you are missing so many other aspects. Many polarities exist, like soft/hard, light/dark, up/down, positive/negative, and masculine/feminine. Somehow the second half of all these pairs got grouped into a category along with evil. The feminine goddess religions, working at night, worshiping Earth below, and all their animal god consorts, got equated with devils and demons.

The opposite polarity of God, the Great Spirit, is not the Devil. The creator is an all-encompassing divine being, with no beginning, end, or opposite. I choose to look at the divine polarity as masculine and feminine, father and mother, God and Goddess. To consider the Devil as the opposite of God gives it too much power, power most religions with an all-powerful God insist the Devil does not have. The whole idea calls into question the belief of such an evil entity as a whole.

Games Spirits Play

Do not misunderstand me. I do believe in harmful forces in the universe. I believe in a need for protection and awareness. I believe in entities who have fallen away from any connection with life and the creative force. Evil exists, but evil comes from fear and anger, the absence of love and forgiveness.

As we play the games of life on this level of existence, the material world, other beings play their own games, all throughout the universe. If and when they interact with humanity, they play off our own fear and images of evil, assuming names and forms from our collective concepts of evil. Spirits appear as devils, demons, and other nightmarish creatures. They play on our movie mythology and horror novels. Demons come from disenchanted spirits seeking a power they never had.

Do not relinquish any of your power to such entities. They do not force you into harm unless you choose it. Do not give them that much credit. Simply leave them to their games. When they run out of players, they will get bored and find new games.

Our Very Own Demons

Demons are also the manifestation of our own inner trials, our own personal demons—our shadow selves. In times of stress, healing, release, or more enlightenment, we confront our darker aspects to heal them, make peace with them, or release them. Protection methods work equally well for self-created manifestations and unwanted visitors. In my experience, most psychic attacks and demons are manifestations of fear. Others are initiations, to build our confidence under extreme situations.

◎ GHOSTS AND LONELY SOULS ◎

Spirits we discern as unhelpful fall into the demons and devils category or they are spirits who were once in body but got stuck on the way to the next life. These lonely souls are the ghosts and haunts of popular myth.

When a body dies, the essence, the animating force, leaves it and usually travels to the next realm. Guides lead the way to whatever is next. For people who deny death, fear it, seek revenge, or have a very strong bond to the living, like not wanting to leave a family, the essence can stick around the material plane. Their own desires prevent them from identifying with the spirit realm beyond the veil, and such spirits get immersed in the physical, but without a body. They forget where the openings to the veil are, and the deeper they become entrenched in the material world, the more frustrated they become. Usually no one can see them or hear them and they cannot move things. Some manifest enough personal willpower to make themselves seen, heard, or actually move objects. Psychics are particularly sensitive to them, but at times, anyone can see them.

Harmless Entities

Usually these beings mean no harm. They are lost, confused, and unhappy. They need someone to help them. They can loose their personality and consciousness completely over time. In their frustration and anger they cause harm or become immersed in the darker emotions of anger, hate, and fear. They spread these "vibes" throughout their dwelling, giving the feeling of a haunted house. Most ghosts become fixated on a particular area, building, or home, usually where they lived or died. Some create their own personal version of hell on the lower vibrations of the astral when stuck between worlds.

The best thing to do with ghosts or any other harmful entities is to offer them a way to the light. Ask your guides for help and visualize a portal of light opening. Fill the rooms with light. Tell the being it is forgiven, although forgiveness is an alien concept to most. These beings may wholeheartedly thank you or reject you completely. Do not force them, but ask them to go where it would be for their highest good. Personal protection techniques are discussed in the next section.

Hauntings

Hauntings can actually lack any form of consciousness. Particularly powerful images can get trapped in the ethers of an area, creating images like ghost battlefields or a person walking down a flight of stairs. You have no interaction with the apparition, since there is nothing there. Imagine a recording, in this case, a holographic recording, being played over and over again. Many spirits are only the shells of the soul, the lower etheric and astral bodies, remaining cohesive long after the true soul departs. Part of their energy refuses to dissipate and be claimed by the natural cycles or restructure. These lower vibrational bodies roam around mindless and zombielike, creating the apparition effect.

Very rarely you will find a ghost happy to be a ghost. Usually, it is a being who has not adjusted to its new condition, but because it fears crossing over it is happy to observe things from where it is. This sort of soul is not attached to a specific place, but takes an interest in a person, usually a relative or friend. I know someone who has a guide in this category. I do not know what kind of guidance he gets, but I imagine it might be like talking to a friend. The ghost has some greater perspective, but not the perspective of one who has crossed over the veil. I imagine the fear that holds it back would also taint the guidance to some degree.

On the whole, haunted homes and disembodied spirits are rare. Most of the eerie feeling at supposedly haunted spots is due to residues of harmful energy, often from families, events, psychic "pollution," or improper alignment with the energy lines of the land. Unfortunately, most architects do not practice feng shui, and buildings are not always built in accord with the land, thus setting up traps and pockets for energy to settle. The energy absorbs imprints from strong emotions, and residents continually pass through these pockets of imprinted energy that give the feeling of bad "vibes" or a malevolent force.

◎ PROTECTION ◎

When doing any deep metaphysical work, play it smart and have some form of protection. Particularly with spirit work, there is the possibility of meeting a being who does not have your highest good in mind or is not capable of giving you beneficial energy even with the best of intentions. I hate using the words *negative* or *positive* when dealing with spirits or thoughts. In popular usage positive is "good" and negative is "bad," but each word denotes a charge, like an electrical charge. If you have too much of a positive charge, you are as out of balance as with too much negative charge. I prefer the words *harmful, unwanted, unbalanced,* or *discordant energy* instead of *negative*. In any case, you need protection from what will harm you.

First Defenses

We have touched upon a few protection methods. With automatic writing and pendulums, if you get some spirit who makes you uncomfortable, stop. If their energy persists, you banish them three times, using the names of God/Goddess/Great Spirit. Use white light to fill the room, and call upon your guardian spirits. If you are specifically unaware of your guardian spirit's name, simply call upon your guardian spirit to protect you.

Incense

A more physical action is to burn incense. Several kinds of incense raise the vibration of an area, forcing lower-level spirits, things we consider harmful, to either raise their vibration and intent accordingly, or leave. These scents are used the world over to create temple space, a sacred area. No harmful beings would bother an act of worship while the incense burned. High-vibration incenses include a mixture of frankincense and myrrh or sage, cedar, sweet grass, copal, lavender, and cinnamon. All these things raise the energy to a higher, purer state and are readily available. They come in cones, sticks, and wands, or you can burn the raw substance on self-igniting charcoal available at metaphysical shops. Using the actual substance is my favorite method, but it can be messy. Incense acts the same way white light does, but doing something physical is more reassuring to people not confident about their inner technology. The substance has an inherent power that keeps working, leaving you free to do other things. Before lighting it, bless the incense with your intention of sacred space and protection.

Symbols

Symbols are protective. You can have a medallion made into a protective symbol. The cross, pentacle, ankh, and Eye of Horus are popular protective symbols. Some Germanic and Norse runes are used for protection—draw the symbol in the air in front of you. (See figure 5 on page 96 for examples of protective symbols.)

A banishing pentagram (see figure 6 on page 96) is a five-pointed star drawn by starting at the bottom left-hand corner with the intent to banish. When banishing an entity, tell it to "return to its source." The source of everything is the divine creative spirit. More complex symbols are the Seals of Solomon, which are often commercially available as amulets. A medal of St. Christopher is used to protect travelers. On the Italian side of my family, St. Christopher, along with gold charms of a pepper and the hand

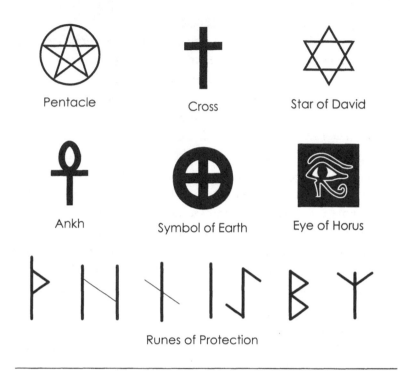

Pentacle   Cross   Star of David

Ankh   Symbol of Earth   Eye of Horus

Runes of Protection

Figure 5. Protective Symbols

Figure 6. Banishing Pentagram

with outstretched index and pinky fingers, are to protect from the evil eye and any curses. Use the symbols resonating with you.

Energy Fields

Everybody is an energy field. It is as much a part of you as your head, leg, or hand. This energy, like all others, can be programmed with intent. With visualizations, spoken word, and intent, the energy can be programmed to protect you from any harmful energy. The program must be constantly reaffirmed, but it works. You are sovereign over your own being. No beings can harm you unless you let them. Sometimes, our higher self puts us into situations for growth and learning. The more in accord you are with your higher self and divine will, the less likely things will happen by surprise, but when working with spirits, these protection methods are well tested.

Although you will rarely encounter harmful beings, each of these techniques will successively bring you a stronger sense of protection. Once you are comfortable doing one, try the next method. I usually use the crystal shield, affirming it daily in my own spiritual practices, but if you should come across something disturbing, invoke the other techniques as a "backup." You can also invoke love of self and love from the creator spirit. One of the strongest tools harmful spirits have is fear. Fear is only the absence of love. It is easy to psych yourself out and give yourself the creeps. Focus on the love.

My Problem Spirits

I have faced only a few harmful spirits, and to this day I cannot say if any one of them was merely harmful or really evil. They made me uncomfortable and my other trusted guides refused to work with them, but remained silent as to their nature. So I chose not to work with them either.

One encounter happened when I was in Los Angeles on a business trip. Environmental factors and pollution could have had an effect, but I found all sorts of strange spirits and psychic phenomenon there. No wonder mediums flock to L.A. One spirit in particular, named Darius, appeared to me. In some ways he was the most intensely physical spirit I have met, and at moments I doubted my sanity because I swear he was physically in my hotel room and we were having a conversation. He was hideous and reptilian, but reminded me of myself on a different evolutionary track. Trust was not my first response. Later he showed me about accepting my dark side with love and has not been back since.

Another spirit, a female reptilian spirit named Adapa, fought me on the astral plane. We never spoke, but somehow I knew her name when I first saw her. Adapa was straight out of the Creature Cantina from *Star Wars*. Reptiles seem to have a thing against me, and now I take their appearance as a warning sign. The encounter felt like a duel as Adapa tried to create energy cords between us, but I am unsure if it was a test or for real, or both. We hit a stalemate, and she left. Although I was unharmed and not corded to her, I felt she was not completely defeated. I guess she got bored with me and left.

The last problem spirit was a dog or jackal. Part of my daily meditation at the time involved opening a portal to another realm and experiencing the pure energy of this realm. As I opened the portal, the animal raced past me and into the door. I knew only those with the ability to open the portal should pass through it. With the help of my guides I stopped the animal. The creature then ran away, refusing to communicate with me. I have been more vigilant ever since. The being was not evil and did not attack, but its presence was unwanted and uninvited. Many practitioners of spirit work have similar experiences and successfully use these techniques to drive away the unwanted.

Though it always pays to be cautious and to know self-defense, you probably will not have to use these methods. We know where the emergency exits are on an airplane, but most people never need them.

EXERCISE 9 – CIRCLE OF LIGHT

❶ Do Exercise 1 to open to a more receptive state if possible. If you feel immediately threatened, you can skip this step. Intent is the most powerful tool.

❷ Say, "I call upon all my spirit allies, guides, and guardians who come in perfect love and perfect trust. I call upon the power of God/Goddess/Great Spirit to protect me."

❸ Draw a ring around yourself and any companions. Visualize a ring of violet-white light forming around you. Say, "I cast this circle to protect us from all forces, positive, negative, or otherwise, that may come to do us harm. Only those who come for our highest good may enter this circle."

The circle of light is a temporary ward against unwanted spirits. Usually this is enough to dispel lower thoughtforms and beings from the area, because you are calling on the Great Spirit. If you or your companions physically cross the boundaries, the circle is broken. The circle can be used in conjunction with incense. Sea salt is sometimes used to mark the boundary circle. It absorbs and grounds harmful energies. The circle of light is the basis of many ritual magic ceremonies and is used commonly by both witches and paranormal investigators.

When you are finished with the circle, you can say, "I cast this circle out into the universe to continue to protect us. The circle is undone, but not broken."

EXERCISE 10 – CRYSTAL SHIELD

❶ Do Exercise 1 to open to a more receptive state if possible.

❷ Visualize the circle of light around you, just beyond your arms' length in all directions.

❸ Visualize the circle expanding up and over your head and below your feet. The light forms a large sphere or egg around you, completely surrounding your body.

❹ Visualize the violet-white light sphere or egg turning into a transparent crystal. It will let in only energy that is correct and good for you. Do not visualize it in opaque colors, since those colors will block light. You are programming your energy to let in only what you want and need, for your highest good.

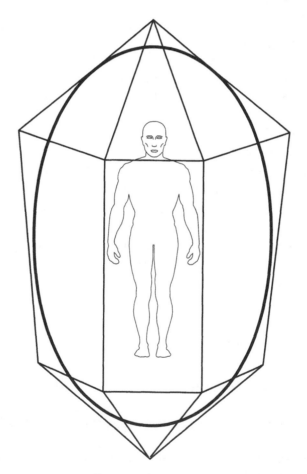

Figure 7. Crystal Shield

❺ Say, "I charge this crystal shield to protect me from all harm on any level and to reflect love back on the source of the harm."

❻ Let the image fade from your mind's eye, confident it is in place around you.

This exercise should be done before working with any spirits in depth. I start my meditations with it. The shield lasts indefinitely, but can be reaffirmed in times of trouble. I find it is a good habit to have. You can have it activated at all times, and have no boundaries. It moves as you move, and people can cross the shield's border without disrupting it.

EXERCISE 11 – PILLAR OF LIGHT

❶ Do Exercise 1 to open to a more receptive state if possible.

❷ Visualize the circle of light around you, just beyond your arms' length in all directions.

❸ Visualize the ring expanding downward into a wall of light, reaching the center of Earth. Ask for the protection of the Earth Mother.

❹ Visualize the ring expanding upward into a wall of light, reaching the Sky Father or heavenly realms. Ask for the protection of the Sky Father.

❺ Imagine the pillar of light around you as an impenetrable wall of love. Anyone wishing you harm cannot break through it. It connects you to the polarity of the divine creator, the mother and father aspects. You are completely safe.

The pillar exercise is good to use when you know you are going into a tough situation, but it can also be a part of your daily practice.

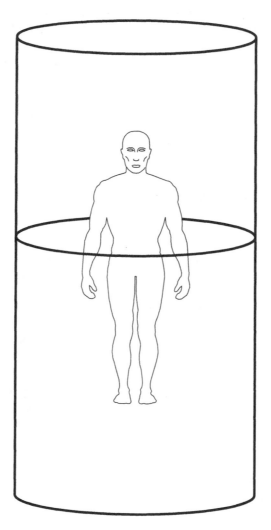

Figure 8. Pillar of Light

There is no need to dispel it because it is part of our own divine nature to be connected to the mother and father aspects of god.

The sky connection can be visualized as many different things, like the Sky Father god or the heavenly kingdom. If you prefer, you can unite with your guardian angel or higher self. Another technique is to connect to the Sun, the source of light and life in this solar system. Many connect to the Christ Consciousness Grid, the energy grid around Earth containing the aspects of unconditional love. All of these techniques work wonderfully.

Another classic defense is to visualize mirrors reflecting energy back to the one who sent it. Some even emphasize and amplify any harmful energy when returning it. While effective, I shy away from this method. I feel it is not my place to make sure that what people send out, comes back to them. That is the universe's function. When I do send something back, I send love and best wishes. I ultimately hope the harmful spirit or person will choose to open to love and no longer want to do or say harmful things. That is the ultimate protection, because then there is no longer a threat.

These protective measures are simple. Experiment. There are many variations. Find a method that suits you. Follow your intuition, and ask your guides their opinion.

◎ INNER TEMPLE ◎

The inner temple is the name of your internal place of power. This is your hidden palace, your interior castle or sanctum. Each of us has a place of power, of shelter inside. The visuals of it can be based on an actual physical place you know of or something fantastic and otherworldly. Gardens, forests, lakes, castles, mountains, pyramids, and fairy mounds are strong images. If I were to place the energy of the inner temple in the physical body, I think it would be in the heart. Love is the key to power, and all power must be tempered with love.

While in your sanctum, you are at the heart of your power. Only those whom you invite can enter. In dreams and meditation you visit it. If someone guides you to a place inside where you feel comfortable, safe, and happy, the first image you get is your inner temple. The image can change and develop as you change, particularly in details, but in essence it will always be your center. The inner temple is one of the best places to meet your allies. By invit-ing only those who are correct and good for you into this space, no others are admitted. Only those who come in love will enter. Discernment is much easier in your place of power, since only you have sovereignty over your body and inner temple.

Think about your place of power. What image makes you feel comfortable? Reflect on it, but do not design your place of power. In the next meditation, it will come effortlessly and unconsciously. Flow with the experience.

◎ RITUAL ◎

Ritual is a great way to meet your allies, since ceremony catalyzes intent and energy, projecting them out into the universe. Rituals let the universe, and the divine, know what you want and need. Many rituals are for marking a turning point in life. They celebrate when a child has become an adult, when a couple intends to join for life, or when a life's journey has come to an end. Ritual can tell the uni-verse you are ready to find a new and better job or you are now releasing a bad relationship.

Rituals are important ceremonies. The very act of ceremony has power to it. Modern Western society is finally remembering the power in heartfelt ceremony. Ritual can even let your allies know you are now ready, willing, and able to meet them.

◎ To be ready is to prepare all your needed skills. If you are work-ing on opening your psychic skills or have previous talent and experience, then you will be ready for the meeting. Make sure you know the discernment and protection techniques.

◎ To be willing is to consciously and willfully ask spirit contact to manifest in your life. It is like opening a door that could change your life forever.

◎ To be able is to actually go out and do something that will allow your allies to connect to you. The avenue is up to you. It can be contemplative meditation, shamanic journey, vision quest, lucid dreaming, or deepening your automatic writing skills. Most common is meditation, just quieting the mind and being recep-tive. Divine with a pendulum or muscle testing, asking for guid-ance as to which of the possible avenues is best for you at this time. Let the answer come, even if it is not what you would have chosen.

Create a ritual for yourself, incorporating this path discovered through divination. If you are familiar with ritual already, go ahead and make the ceremony fit your current system. If not, here is a sample ritual to get your mind rolling, using meditation as the means of connection.

EXERCISE 12 – RITUAL TO MEET YOUR FIRST ALLY

❶ Do Exercise 1 to open to a receptive state.

❷ Do any of the protection exercises (Exercises 9, 10, or 11).

❸ Light a white candle to represent the one spirit running through all things. You wish to connect further to spirit through your allies. You can have with you any sacred power objects you have, like crystals, feathers, or ritual tools.

❹ Say, "I ask in the name of the God/Goddess/Great Spirit to be with me here and now. I ask to connect to my spirit allies. I invoke my guides and guardians to be here with me now."

❺ Say, "I ask to connect and openly communicate with the ally who comes in perfect love, trust, and truth and is correct and good for me at this time. So be it and so it is."

⑥ Sit quietly and meditate on your guides, not forcing the experience, but being open. See in your mind's eye a doorway or path leading to a special place sacred to you. It can be somewhere out in nature, like a forest or beach, or more celestial, like golden stairs leading to a heavenly temple. Let the image come to you. This is a place of power for you, your inner temple.

⑦ Ask to see your allies. In your mind's eye, they appear. Or you may feel their presence around your physical body. How do they look or feel? Ask your allies' names. Go with the first impression. They can seem silly at first, but the truth lies with your first impression.

⑧ Ask your allies if they have a message for you at this time. If you meet more than one, you can ask them to speak slowly and one at a time. Ask if this is the truth and comes in love, using the discernment techniques. Ask to feel the love.

⑨ Thank your allies for this experience and return your perception to the physical world. Write down what happened. Things slip away easily when you leave your meditative state.

Go with whatever experience you get. It is the best one for you at this time. Some may have full-fledged conversations with their allies or an intuitive feeling. The message could be nonverbal, a symbolic journey, or a flash of images, colors, sounds, and feelings. Use your discretion. If you have opened the door only a crack, then that is all you are ready to do at this time. There is no right or wrong experience. With each successive contact, the communication will deepen.

Other allies from your spiritual support team are met the same way. Some contact techniques work better for different kinds of spirits. If you work with guides and angels, and really want to connect to your power animal, a shamanic journey using the world tree will be more appropriate. Use drums, rattles, and a more tribal style in your ritual. I have found rose quartz and blue lace agate, along with rose water misted in the area, are good tools to connect to the angelic realms. A crow feather helped me connect with the crow goddess, Macha. The one I use I found stuck in my bedroom window screen, an obvious sign it was meant for me.

The following chapters give more details on members of the spiritual support team and how you can work with them.

CHAPTER SEVEN

PLAYING TWENTY QUESTIONS WITH SPIRIT GUIDES

SPIRIT GUIDES ARE LIKE LONG-LOST friends. In fact, they probably are old friends, beings we have known in this world or the next who stay across the veil. They are drawn to us and agree to guide us while we are on this Earthwalk because we need the support. They love us and wish to see us succeed in our self-chosen mission, our life games.

◎ RELATIONSHIPS WITH SPIRIT GUIDES ◎

Prior relationship is generally the rule, but some guides are brand-new in this lifetime. Our planet and time are attracting a lot of attention from all realms of life, and many who cannot physically be a part of it are interacting in other ways, including agreeing to be spirit guides. If you believe you are a separate and distinct soul before birth and choose what body, place, time, and parents you have, as I believe, then you probably make an agreement with your guides before being born. Even if you plan on having a life where you will not remember or consciously access your guides, you can agree your guide will never speak unless directly spoken to and the guidance comes through intuition and synchronicity. Most people do this, since the majority of the population are unaware of their guides. The support is there, even for those who do not know such help exists.

Like any friend you have not seen in years, you need to rebuild your relationship. Things seem familiar, but your conscious mind has to get reacquainted with the being and your history. How can you take the advice of someone you do not know intimately? If a complete stranger, loving and well intentioned, tells you that you should stop doing x and start doing y, you would tell her to get lost. If your best friend tells you the same thing, you would listen, because you know and trust your friend. The advice is trustworthy. With spirit guides, it is the same. Never listen to someone you do not know. If you test the waters and take the time to know each other, the advice is meaningful.

◎ THE METHODS OF SPIRIT GUIDES ◎

Spirit guides are there to aid you, plain and simple. Since everything in life is spiritual, do not feel there are things off limits for your guide. It never hurts to ask. Money, career, and sex are all valid issues to bring up to your guides. You don't need to feel embarrassed. Be open. Talk about your family driving you crazy, or your boss who is unreasonable. If you had mastered all these realms completely, you would not need guidance in the first place. Immediate enlightenment may not be available, but spirit guides help us see the light.

Particularly talented guides will use a method of guidance suited to you. They can talk like a friend, show you pictures, or take you on a journey through your life, like Scrooge's ghosts of Christmas Past, Present, and Future. Guides sometimes manifest before particularly difficult circumstances in your life to show you they support you while you have these experiences. Farsighted spirits predict your future accurately.

My guides use humor to get a point across. Laughter is a great expression of love, and it helps us open our hearts to a different view. If you tend to be a recovering perfectionist or take yourself too seriously, humor diffuses a delicate situation, transforming it into a fun one. Life is pretty ridiculous, anyway. Spirit allies help me see that, and more importantly, enjoy it.

Guides can lead you down an untrue path. They do not lie to you, but will let you come to your own wrong conclusions to help point out a mistake. They make you think.

Guides are not perfect either. They can be wrong or see things differently from you. They are individuals and make mistakes, or we simply do not agree with them.

Guides will never make you think, do, or say anything you don't want to do. A true spirit ally respects the law of free will. We all have free will, including all spirits, but to be qualified to guide, the spirit must understand and honor this fact. You have a choice in everything you do; ultimately you are responsible for what you do. "Because the voices told me to," does not excuse any action. You must discern and see if it fits you. Just because a guide tells you something does not mean you have to do it. They have a different perspective from you, but they are not omnipotent. You must decide. This is your life.

As with all relationships, you must set your own boundaries. Your sense of space and time is different from most guides. Some understand and remember what it is like in a body. Others have no clue. They get excited when you are finally speaking to them and they wake you up at three in the morning to discuss new information. Kindly tell them never to wake you up when you are sleeping unless you are in danger. The same goes when they are speaking to you at work. If it is awkward to talk, tell them. Feelings will not be hurt. They will respect your limits, but you must set them.

◎ QUESTIONS AND ANSWERS ◎

When you first meet your guides, you might have no immediate concerns or worries. Your relationships and career are going fine.

You have found your path. What do you say? "Now that we've met, I don't understand why I need you?" Cultivate a relationship so you will know and trust your guides when you do need spiritual guidance. Believe me, you will probably need their support from time to time, no matter how great your life is going now.

Here is a series of questions you can ask your guides. They serve to introduce you to each other, satisfy curiosity, dispel fear, and get into whatever issues you have together. The list of questions comes first. Ask them of your guides before looking at my comments, which only reflect my own experiences and the possibilities brought to me by others. Do not let them limit you.

Come and play a game of twenty questions. Do not be surprised if your spirit guides have a list of questions waiting for you.

EₓERCIₛE 13 – TWENTY QUESTIONS

Do this exercise only if you have met an ally you would consider as a spirit guide. If you have first met a power animal or other being that does not speak with you, you can skip ahead to those chapters more appropriate for you at this time or do an intention ritual from chapter 6 to specifically find a spirit guide.

Enter a receptive meditative state by doing Exercise 1. Do any of the protection exercises you feel drawn to do. Then call out to your guide three times. When you lack a name for your guide, ask for the "spirit guide who comes in perfect love and trust, completely correct for me at this time." Then use the discernment techniques from Chapter Six. The set of twenty questions can be broken down into smaller sessions as needed.

❶ *What is your name?*

❷ *What is your purpose?*

❸ *What do you have to tell me?*

❹ *What are you?*

⑤ *Where are you from?*

⑥ *Have you ever lived in a physical body?*

⑦ *Have you lived on Earth?*

⑧ *Do we have any past-life associations?*

⑨ *Do you guide anyone else who is in body?*

⑩ *Do you have an area of expertise, and if so, what is it?*

⑪ *What is the best way to contact you?*

⑫ *How will I recognize you in the future?*

⑬ *Where are you? Are you physically near me at all?*

⑭ *Are you ever "not with me"?*

⑮ *How do I know you are "real" and not a figment of my imagination?*

⑯ *What is my life's purpose?*

⑰ *What is the meaning of life?*

⑱ *What should I be changing in my life?*

⑲ *What can I specifically be doing to improve my health, balance, and overall life?*

⑳ *Why are you my guide? And why are we meeting now, at this point in my life?*

Here are some thoughts that reflect the possible answers guides give and where you are coming from when asking such questions. Ask your guides only the questions to which you want answers. Use this list to inspire your own twenty questions session.

❶ *What is your name?*

❷ *What is your purpose?*

❸ *What do you have to tell me?*

The first questions are introductory. They are probably the first questions you would naturally ask your guides. If the answers are unclear, ask them to communicate more directly or in a manner you will be able to hear.

Basically, you want to know with whom you are working and if you resonate with them. Names, particularly in magic, are very important. Age-old magicians say if you have a thing's true name, then you have power over it. Mages would adopt a magical name and tell no one, so no one would have power over them. You do not have power over that being, but you do get a fundamental insight into the spirit. Some names seem strange or silly to us, since they are translations into our language from the nonspeaking realms and there is not a satisfactory equivalent.

Power syllables including *ma, ra, ka, om, us, os, is, la, le, lo, at,* and *eem* are found in a being's true names. Think of the beings from the most ancient mythologies like Ra, Isis, Horus, Kali, Pele, Macha, Hera, Hecate, and Tiamat. They all have these powerful sounds in their name. Personal magical names incorporate these sounds.

Once you know its name, determine the guide's purpose and specifically what it wants with you. Discern the general feeling of the spirit and its intentions. If spirit or message is dubious, ask for proof.

The next batch of seven questions is based on our own curiosity about spirits and guides. They are for getting our feet wet before going into more meaningful discussion, but the answers can be illuminating and eventually become the basis of our own personal cosmology.

❹ *What are you?*
Answers range from any of the possibilities mentioned in chapters 2 and 3 to something different and unexpected. Be open to all possibilities.

❺ *Where are you from?*
The origin of our spirit ally is very important. This is a place for

strong discernment. If you are working in the Norse traditions, you may get Asgard or one of the other Norse nine worlds for an answer. Guides from Celtic traditions come from Avalon. Spirits from Eastern traditions hail from Shamballa. If working in the light-worker cosmology, your answer could be Sirius because your guide is from that star system. Expect as many different answers as you have guides.

❻ *Have you ever lived in a physical body?*
This question helps us put into perspective any advice given on the physical body and the crazy things we do here on Earth. If the spirit has no prior experience, it has a hard time relating to things like sex, money, or chocolate chip ice cream. Health issues are difficult to understand, because in its reality, you manifest what you need. We do, too, but the lag time between intention and physical reality is longer for us.

Linear time is another difficulty for spirits with no previous experience with it. Time is really cyclical, but to beings in a body, it appears to go from point A to B to C. This viewpoint is lacking in many spirits, but if they were in a body, they have a greater under-standing of our current perception. If they never were in a body, it does not mean their advice is automatically unworthy, just remember the source. You could have another guide who is more appro-priate for your physical arena.

❼ *Have you lived on Earth?*
Like the question above, this information helps us understand the guide's perspective and how it relates to our life on Earth. Being in a body somewhere else can be different, and yes, I am told there are many places where one can be in a body. Earth is not the exclusive home for the physical. It helps to ask if it has been in a human body. Your spirit could have incarnated as a different life-form.

❽ *Do we have any past-life associations?*
You are linked to your guide for any number of reasons. In past lives,

the two of you may have been together in a physical relationship, as family members, lovers, or enemies. As part of an agreement on the higher level of consciousness, one being has agreed to guide the other, or you may have been the guide for your current ally when she was in a body. Offering aid as a spirit guide and ally is one way of transmuting and releasing karma with another person or a way to continue your love and commitment beyond the veil. Family members and older ancestor spirits often counsel a family or clan. Partly it is a debt to the family and partly a desire to help loved ones.

❾ *Do you guide anyone else who is in body?*
Spirit guides cannot cheat on you. They are not bonded to one and only one person. They may be working with several people, consciously or unknowingly, across time and space. People with similar spiritual backgrounds, friends, and family members might all be working with the same group of guides or have allies in common. My guide Asha told me the list of whom she works with is too large to name. If she had to wait for me to talk to her, she would be bored. When I asked my guardian angel Arak if he guarded anyone else, he told me "No. Currently, you are the only embodied being on Earth I am guarding." To me those words implied that, as a being beyond space and time, he has had other charges at other times, places, and levels of reality.

❿ *Do you have an area of expertise, and if so, what is it?*
Everybody comes into your life for a reason, including spirit guides. They each have a purpose. Some are general life guides, but others have specific functions.

Asha is a general guide for me and is most like my regular friends. We can talk and share experiences without a purpose. She gives advice without making it a big spiritual event. Often she just gives common sense. Her higher purpose is to help me with emotional work and healing. She is also my Reiki guide.

I saw her in a meditation while taking my second-level Reiki training. Expecting a different guide, I was surprised to find my familiar friend. When I asked her what she was doing there, she told me that she was initiated into many healing arts, both when she was in a body and in other realms, and that she is here to help me with Reiki and many other healing methods.

Reiki guides are those spirits who are responsible for bringing Reiki healing, the universal life force, back into widespread use. Some of the earliest practitioners of the healing art have now gone on to become Reiki guides. Everyone who is attuned to the healing energy of Reiki gets the attention of at least one Reiki guide, but most are unaware of it. Reiki practitioners sometimes feel the presence of guides when healing and attuning new healers.

Reiki attunements work through the process of sacred symbols of healing energy. During my attunement, Asha explained two other Reiki symbols I received for my personal use. She guides all my sessions in partnership with me and sometimes introduces me to my clients' healing guides.

My other main guide, Llan, works with me through information and training. He tells me technical things, sharing information I would normally not have. Lately, he has backed off from the pure information and shares some things in a story format. He leaves me to decide if these myths actually happened or if they are only a vehicle for teaching.

Macha is with me whenever I am teaching witchcraft. She asked me to start teaching and she remains my guide, companion, and protector in these situations. I find her sometimes guiding the class if someone needs to hear something specific I did not plan on covering. After taking my classes, many people feel a connection to her.

Other areas of expertise are not necessarily that structured. A person I talked to while researching this book reported having a laughing guide, one who really reminded her to take life less seriously. Although I have never called him a laughter guide, one of the ascended masters I work with always brings me back to love through laughter. He times things just right, usually showing up when my world seems its darkest or right before things hit the fan.

Laughter guides are becoming more common, particularly for guides coming from the Land of Faery.

Guides act in a counselor capacity, or as healers, both spiritual and physical. They come for creative inspiration and partnership, particularly for artists and musicians, but every field needs a boost of creativity now and then. Muses are the spirits of inspiration, named in Greek mythology. They visit artists and poets to inspire new work. Dream guides work exclusively with their people in the sleep states. Let the spirits come to you with their talents. If you have a specific need or desire, request a guide with expertise in that area–it's okay to make an "appointment." Make a list of the qualities you want in a guide and use that as part of your intention and contact ritual.

The following questions come from our fear of the intangibility of spirit relationships. When someone is not physical, you cannot go over to his house and knock on the door. For one not used to it, or unsure of his own psychic abilities, the connection seems nebulous at best. You fear your guide will not be there when you need him, will not answer you calls, or will not even hear them. These questions try to quell the fears in such a relationship. You never know what others are feeling unless you ask and tell them how you feel.

⓫ *What is the best way to contact you?*
We each have our spiritual 911 to the forces of the universe. We may forget how to tune the receiver, but the parts still work. Guides give us simple, reassuring methods to help us connect with them. The techniques can be as simple as closing your eyes and saying their name three times silently.

⓬ *How will I recognize you in the future?*
Discernment techniques are very important and reassuring, but eventually you will come to recognize your spirit allies from their energy. When you were a child, people looked a lot alike, but you knew who loved you by their presence. You learn a similar recognition skill with your guides. They have specific speech patterns, ways

of addressing you, mannerisms, and in general, unique "vibes." Some mischievous spirits pick up such things from your mind. They use telepathy to gain the information, but the impersonation will never be exact. The act lacks the original's love and emotion. Whenever you are in doubt, use the discernment techniques. Even when you are not in doubt, test yourself and your connection. That way you will better gauge your future responses when in a tense situation.

13 *Where are you? Are you physically near me at all?*

14 *Are you ever "not with me?"*
Where do guides go when we are not talking with them? Where do they live? Not easy questions and best left up to your own guides to answer. I feel the physical sensation of my guides. Macha is mostly behind me, Asha is on one side, and Llan on the other. The spider totems seem to be everywhere around me. Other guides do not have such a physical presence to them.

I have been told our guides are always with us, or at least in earshot of a psychic call. While they are guiding us, they have different aspects to their life on their own plane of existence. As beings beyond linear time, they can do many things simultaneously and interrelate them.

15 *How do I know you are "real" and not a figment of my imagination?*
Imagination is the first explanation of spirits. The experience is all taking place in the mind. To a certain extent, this is true. I first heard my allies' voices in my own head. Any physical sensation I have is right above my ears, or on the top or crown of my head. Sometimes the communication is in my own internal voice and sometimes not. Many beings do not communicate verbally, but to understand their message, we translate it into the closest approximation—we hear it in our own words.

Trust and doubt are two important components of any relationship. The more you trust not only in your guide, but yourself and the universe, the less doubt you will have. This is a hard task indeed, but well worth it. We all have moments of doubt, particu-larly being raised in a modern, Western society where most people never speak to spirits. Our friends look at us funny and we start to think, "Am I gullible? Am I crazy?" You want reassurance that this experience is not a figment of a delusional mind or merely your own internal dialogue. Some might not need that assurance, feeling per-fectly comfortable in the thought they are talking to a wiser aspect of themselves. Others desperately need it.

I went through a period of doubt awhile ago. I asked Asha and Llan, "How do I know I am not crazy? Tell me something I wouldn't ordinarily be aware of so I will know you are an independent being with a different perspective. Give me something I can then prove." That was a tall order. They told me "Steve's mother is blind." I had just met my life partner Steve a few months earlier and I had not met his parents yet. When I did, I could tell his mother saw better than I did. My guides were wrong. I was talking to myself. I stopped calling on Asha or Llan for quite a while. Then I hung out with an old friend named Stephen, whom I used to call Steve. He told me that his mother had been declared legally blind. So my guides were right all along and I was too blind to see. Ironically, they chose an eye problem to help me open my eyes. I went back, and like a good friend, apologized profusely. They laughed. Our relationship changed greatly after that, and they became more of a part of my daily life.

⑯ *What is my life purpose?*

⑰ *What is the meaning of life?*

⑱ *What should I be changing in my life?*

⑲ *What can I specifically be doing to improve my health, balance, and overall life?*

⑳ *Why are you my guide? And why are we meeting now, at this point in my life?*

The final group of questions involves your own work and issues while in a body. I saved them for last because they are the most important. The answers are unique to you and the advice can be simple and practical. A friend's Native American guide told her to hug a pine tree when feeling unbalanced. She does and it works. Her guide also told her to leave a resort that was built on an Indian burial ground. When she ignored the message, all manner of strange occurrences happened. After she left, her friends back at the resort reported everything went back to normal. The story sounds a bit cliché, but superstitions, folktales, and modern legends usually cover a nugget of truth.

Guides want to start with these questions, but for many, you need to build a trusting relationship before you can truly listen to the advice and make hard decisions in life. They are not so hard once you realize you have a whole team behind you. Our missions in life are only games. Each of us has a game we thought would be fun to play. Guides want to help us play, like a good coach, but the coach cannot play for the team.

This game of twenty questions is just a start. Everyone will have her own questions and answers. What do you need to know? Ask it. No one book, religion, or even guide can give the answer. All answers are within, and spirit guides help you find them by triggering your journey of self-discovery.

CHAPTER EIGHT

FINDING THE ANIMAL WITHIN

EVERYONE WORKS WITH A POWER animal. We all have an animal nature. Our gut feelings and our innate body wisdom are our animal instinct. Although we occasionally have self-doubt when listening to our instinct, animals listen to their instincts and live in harmony with all.

◎ ANIMAL ENERGIES ◎

To those who study the zodiac, our animal nature is apparent. A wheel of stars encircles us. The wheel is divided into twelve groups or constellations. These patterns of stars form pictures most often identified with animals of myth. The term *zodiac* means "wheel of animals" even though a few signs are based on other symbols. Everyone is affected by these stellar, yet animal energies. Various systems of astrology differ in their methods and cultural representations of the animals, but each seems to work in tandem with the others. Each system has similar animals and animal natures. The Taurus bull of Western astrology is similar to the Ox of Chinese astrology.

People express these animal energies differently. Many express not only personality traits, but also physical characteristics. One of my students who is a Leo sun sign, the sign of the lion, has many feline characteristics and mannerisms. She was not surprised to find the cat as her power animal. Other animals in Western astrology are the ram, bull, crab, horse, scorpion, goat, and fish. We each have these energies, but express them differently. Truly a kingdom of animals exists within us not limited to the zodiac. Animal energies come in every form. They embody who we are and who we want to become.

Through the physical animal's natural instincts, tendencies, and characteristics, the power animal brings its wisdom, called medicine. Each animal brings a different medicine that "cures" humanity's tendencies to live out of balance. To get an idea about an animal's medicine, look at its habits. What do its actions symbolize to you?

Consider the snake. This poor creature has been much maligned in history. The snake is not a symbol of the devil and temptation, but of the Goddess. Banishing the snake from the Garden of Eden or the British Isles was the banishment of the Goddess. The snake crawls on its belly and so is close to Mother Earth. The snake's whole body is in constant communion with the mother. It slithers like the waves of the ocean, or the magnetic fields of Earth. Waves in all forms carry energy. The very shape of the snake is a sign of the God, being long and phallic, a symbol of the Earth Lord's virility. Skin is shed, removing the old, dead, and unwanted so the new, fresh skin can live. As we change and grow, we must remove what does not serve. Snakes are regeneration and healing. All this wisdom is inherent in the daily life of the snake.

Each animal has power to show us. Squirrels teach us to prepare for the future just as they prepare for the winter; they work with resources and consolidation. Rams teach adventure and courage. Sea horses show us fidelity–they mate for life–and gender reversal–the male gives birth. Mosquitoes work with us on fear, annoyance, and our own irritations. If snakes share regeneration, butterflies teach complete transformation of the self. Wolves protect, as they are fiercely protective about the pack; through them we learn to care for those around us. The list is endless. Every single animal has a lesson to teach.

Many power animals no longer roam the Earth physically. They wander the astral realms between here and the veil of other realities. These creatures are the monsters of myth and legend or those who have passed on through extinction. You may find your totem to be the unicorn, griffin, or dragon. Each works in the realm of magic. The unicorn's horn was once a prized mythic magical ingredient, and the creatures are pure of heart and fierce protectors of woman and children. Griffins teach the magic of alchemy, uniting the powers of lion and eagle as a fierce guardian. Dragons are particularly powerful in the world and, like angels, are making their comeback. The ancient Chinese culture knows their power, naming the lines of energy running across Earth dragon lines. Dragons are masters of the five Chinese elements, and often very friendly if asked nicely for a favor. Some want nothing to do with humans, so use your discretion. The book *Medicine Cards: The Discovery of Power Through the Ways of Animals,* by Jamie Sams and David Carson, is a great resource on the power of animal medicine.

As your psychic abilities and confidence increase, you can directly contact animals found in nature or power animals discovered in meditative journeys. Always look to the physical animal and how it relates to the world. That is how practitioners and mystics get their information on animal medicine. They ask and experience. When you find your own totems, ask them what lessons they have for you. The best way to know their power is to experience it yourself.

EXERCISE 14 – FINDING YOUR POWER ANIMAL

❶ Lie down on your back. Cover your eyes. Get comfortable, but not so comfortable you will fall asleep. Make the intention that this journey will connect you to your animal ally.

❷ Do Exercise 1 to reach a meditative state. Do any of the protective exercises you feel drawn to do. If you have a drumming tape, play it. Choose the shortest selection, five to fifteen minutes. Or have your partner guide you through Exercise 1 and start drumming if you are using live music.

❸ In your mind's eye, picture a very large tree, with roots digging into the earth and branches rising up high in the sky. This is the world tree.

❹ Imagine this picture on the screen of your mind as a window. Open the window and step through. You are standing before the world tree.

❺ Look for an opening near the tree. It can be in the roots or in the trunk or next to the tree, like a hole or dark pool of water.

❻ Enter the opening and explore the tunnel. It is like the birth canal into the next world. You may feel you are ascending to the upper world or descending to the lower world. Follow your intuition.

❼ Look for a light at the end of the tunnel. Go out into this new world. Take note of the scenery and what you encounter. Treat everything with great respect and reverence. An animal guide immediately greets you. It may speak directly to you, or more likely show you things through a journey. Ask any questions you have and wait for the answers. Follow your instincts and inner voice.

❽ If you are not greeted by an animal guide, any animal you see more than four times that appears friendly is your power animal. Try to make contact with it. If unsuccessful, you are not ready for contact and can try again later.

❾ Return to the trunk of the world tree, the middle world, by the same tunnel you came down.

❿ Return your perceptions back to the room. Make and speak the intention, "I release all that does not serve," three times. This releases any unwanted or harmful energies you have picked up on your journey.

Now you have made first contact with your animal spirit ally. Think about anything the animal showed you and how it affects you life. What is the nature of the animal itself? Does it resonate with things already in you or things you should be learning?

◎ ANIMAL SPIRIT ALLIES ◎

The words *power animal, totem,* and *familiar* are often used inter-changeably. They each mean an animal spirit ally. *Power animal* is a more general term, not as evocative of past traditions but empha-sizing the natural energy of each animal form and archetype. *Totem* comes from the more tribal traditions of North, South, and Central America and Siberia. Not only do individual people have totems, but tribes have totems too.

Familiars

Familiar is the term used by European witches. It differs slightly from totems and power animals as these terms usually refer strictly to spiritual allies. Seeing their physical counterpart is considered a good omen or message. A familiar is a single, specific animal in the physical world. The spirit of the ally can reside in the animal's body, as the natural occupant, or in a blended consciousness when the familiar is not working in the spiritual realms. For example, a cat spirit ally "lives" in your cat Moonstar when not shamanically working with you in other realms. It could be Moonstar's animal soul or an addition to Moonstar's soul. The process is similar to magical spirits "living" in statues, objects, crystals, or the proverbial magic lamp. The familiar is Moonstar, your cat, not every cat you see. Spirit allies choose to do this to live and work more closely with you. I have several colleagues who feel their pets are advanced spirits doing their own work in animal form to help the planet and the humans with whom they connect. Dogs, horses, and rabbits have shattered the traditional image of the black cat and the toad as the only familiars.

You most likely have a primary animal ally, like a primary spirit guide. It embodies many lessons you need to learn. As you connect with your animal, you soon identify with it. Your essence takes on more of its characteristics.

One of my first totems was Crow, through my connection with Macha. She is both a crow and a horse goddess, but she appears to me mostly in her crow aspect, with a dark, feathered cloak. I would see crows everywhere when I started working with her. They would flock in my yard, and only my yard, not the neighbors'. Even though I knew Crow was my totem, it was still strange at first. A friend and student of mine did a ritual and asked for my spiritual aid and presence while she was alone. A crow landed and looked at her right after she asked for my higher self to be with her. The crow stayed until her ritual was over, and then promptly left after she thanked it.

The second animal ally I found was Spider, but Spider really found me. I was bitten by one as a child, had an allergic reaction to it, and was rushed to the emergency room. The event did not imme-diately precipitate my fear of spiders, and I consider it my first ini-tiation into the spider world in this lifetime.

My aversion to spiders emerged much later, after college. Suddenly, I saw spiders everywhere. They were in my house, room, car, and at friends' homes too. They would show up only when I was around. I ignored them; just a coincidence, I thought. I tried not to be afraid. Then the spiders got trickier. They would not be ignored. They would climb to the corner of the wall and ceiling, get right above my head, then fall onto me. It happened several times, and I was seriously freaked out.

Then, one night, watching TV home alone on my bed, I felt a presence. Whenever anything similar happened before, I usually wrote it off as my imagination. This time it was too strong. I could see a shadow out of the corner of my eye, but when I looked, it would disappear. I looked up for spiders. There were none. I relaxed. I tend to have good visual experiences when I meditate or journey, but I am not one who usually sees visions. Suddenly, there it was, a giant spider, intangible and ghostlike, in my doorway. From tip to tip it was five feet long. Saw it, ignored it. My mind was play-ing tricks on me. Then it leaped from the doorway to me, pinning me down. I physically moved! I could see what I called the "astral spider" over me. I think I could have closed my eyes and stopped the experience if I wanted, but I did not think to do so. The expe-rience was gruesome, and I was in a bit of a shock, to say the least. In a deep metallic voice the creature basically said to get over it. Spiders will not hurt me if I leave them alone. They teach handling fear and creation and writing. Then it disappeared. The whole thing seems far-fetched. I know it was not a physical occurrence. I was in an altered state. I never realized you could be so deep in trance and have your eyes wide open.

I thought this vision would culminate my experience, but since then spiders, both physical and astral, have been drawn to me. I see them in my meditations and journeys and feel their presence when I write this. Their webs guide my path. I have been up in the branches of the world tree and been honored to meet Spider Grandmotherfather. Through past-life regressions I discovered blurred images of a spider cult in ancient times. When I see a spi-der now, I know I am being asked to contact my spider guides. As soon as I acknowledge this, they disappear. Your own introduction to power animals does not have to be this dramatic.

Many animal spirits visit me now. In particular is a dolphin ally named Shasha. Unlike many other totems, which feel so archetypal and encompassing the entire species, Shasha has an individual name and distinct personality. I feel she could be a real living, breathing dolphin somewhere in the world that astrally projected to join with me. Her origin remains uncertain because I forgot to ask. The details were not important at the time. Shasha helped me salvage the best from a bad situation in the deep waters of my subconscious. After I got laid off from an unhealthy job, she helped me wash away the bad and look to the good of the situation and my experience there. I have not seen her since.

The coatl, the feathered serpent in Aztec mythology, is a fre-quent ally. Many birds with their long plumes are mistaken for the coatl. A great snake with feathery wings and scales, the coatl does not exist in the physical world, but in the spirit realms this animal is quite real. He guides many of my journeys.

Your animal spirit is often your guide when you journey through the shamanistic worlds above and below. It does not usually offer advice like a traditional image of a spirit guide, but it will take you where you need to go and protect you.

Shamanic journeys bring back energy. The energy can be knowl-edge or pure power used to heal or accomplish your goal. If you have a need, illness, or question, you can journey for the answer. Beings in the spirit realms or your own experiences are there to help solve the problem. Spirit herbs gathered in an otherworldly garden, brewed in a potion, have healed me in the spirit world, which then translated into the physical. Follow your ally and your own instincts.

Invoking Your Animal Ally's Help

Follow the previous exercise, 14, but replace the intention to find your animal ally with an intention to solve a problem, gain infor-mation, heal, or succeed in a task. Invoke your animal ally's help. The visualizations in this type of journey are spontaneous. They cannot be planned out in steps like other exercises. If you have recurring migraine headaches, your intention could be, "I seek a complete cure for my headaches in the other realms. I ask my ani-mal guide, the _____, to aid me in this task for my highest good." If you need extra power to complete a paper you are writing for English class, your intention may be, "I ask for the power to suc-cessfully complete my English term paper and invoke my animal allies to bring me to this power safely and for my highest good." Always include something about your goal being good for you or harming none. Journeys with totems bring encounters with your other spirit allies, angels, or deities in these realms. Your own belief system colors the character of your experience.

You can also modify Exercise 8 to do a dream journey with your animal ally using your intention to solve a problem or seek power you need. The dream will offer a symbolic solution to your quest or rejuvenate you. Make sure to relax yourself sufficiently before bed. Try these special bedtime rituals: Relax the mind with quiet music or incense. Use essential oils like lavender to calm and soothe. Light a candle, but make sure to extinguish it before crawling into bed. A rested and receptive mind will be able to journey in the dream state.

You have now learned the basic skills and can go forward from here. Experiment. Each journey, like every life, is unique.

CHAPTER NINE

CALLING ON PROTECTIVE SPIRITS

GUARDIANS COME IN MANY shapes and sizes. Any spirit who has adopted the role of protector is your guardian. They are the easiest spirits to call. Even people who are not involved with any metaphysical discipline usually believe in them, in one form or another, like guardian angels. Everyone has the talent to call them. Their names are not necessary, though that helps. Shamanistic or psychic skills are not required. All you need is intention.

Intention takes many forms and is commonly the form most natural to you. If you are good with words, speaking is your form of call. Call your guardian spirit to be with you. You can speak silently to yourself or out loud if that seems more commanding. You can visualize your guardian coming to protect you. Or you can simply intend your guardian to be with you. They respond to our thoughts. No fancy call or visuals are needed, but they are tools to help us with intent.

◎ PROTECTION FROM PHYSICAL HARM ◎

Guardian spirit allies protect us on many levels. The first and most obvious level of protection is physical. Guardians are called in times of crisis to protect us from physical harm. You are not exempt from invoking your own protective powers. Your protection shield (see Exercise 10, chapter 6) protects you from all harm, not just dangerous spirits. If you are traveling, invoke your guardians to be with you and your traveling companions. If you are doing anything even remotely dangerous, call your protective spirits to be with you. If you are unaware of their names, simply ask for your guardian spirits, for your guardian angel, or for complete protection from the God/Goddess/Great Spirit. Protection will come.

Just before writing this section I heard from a friend whose loved one had been in a serious car accident. The victim's thoughts moments before the crash were of my friend and her talk about angels always being there to help. With this in mind, he called on his guardian angel to protect him. He survived with some injuries, but considering the damage to his car, medics were baffled as to how he could be intact. This person had no background in metaphysics, meditation, or magic, but he successfully called on his angel just the same. In fact, until that moment, he was not even sure he believed in guardian angels. I hear many stories like this when teaching magic and meditation. They often include out-of-body experiences where injured people see or hear angels and spirits around them, helping save them. Sometimes people find white feathers near accident scenes and take them to be physical assurances from angels. My guardians have darker wings, like Macha, so when I find crow feathers I regard them as a sign of protection.

Your guardians protect your physical vessel until it is the right time for you to leave, whether you have finished what you have to do or you have decided on a higher level to leave this life. They seem to not guard against physical disease as much as injury. Most metaphysicians believe all disease is brought on by an individual through "dis-ease," the act of being uneasy, worried, tense, and generally unbalanced by emotion, thought, environment, or diet. Sickness is an attempt of the body to tell us something is wrong. Protective spirit allies work only against seemingly outside influence, although keep in mind we live in an interdependent and connected universe. If we cocreate our own experiences, then nothing is truly outside. Ask your guardians what is in their function to protect.

◎ PROTECTION FROM HARMFUL ENERGIES ◎

We are multilevel beings, not just physical. We have an emotional, mental, and spiritual body too. These bodies can be harmed only by other energies. Thoughts, intentions, magic, psychic attacks, and harmful spirits are all forms of energy. Guardians, along with our own protection exercises, can block these harmful forms of energy from influencing us. They act as psychic gatekeepers who keep unwanted spirits and energies from attacking us in any way. If you do any medium work or channeling, or deal with a lot of different spirits in general, it's good to garner a relationship with your gatekeeper. Make sure you know your own limits and the limits of your gatekeeper. It keeps harmful beings from entering your energy field or your body. This is a particular danger with full-body trance channelers who work with more than one spirit.

In my own work, Macha is my psychic guardian. At every class I teach or attend, I feel her presence strongly. In the physical world, I think my guardian angel, Arak, looks out more for my body. Either is capable of handling both arenas very well, but at this time, I get the impression of the two of them at work. In the beginning, I only knew Macha, so I assumed she alone was protecting me.

The important thing to know is guardian spirits are in no way completely responsible for your safety. We have talked about your role in creating your reality. You have a hand in everything that happens to you, be it on a conscious or a higher level. With the protection techniques you have learned, you have rights and sovereignty over your being.

Even though it is unnecessary to know your guardian spirit's name, since everyone has one, it certainly helps you build a relationship. Other spirit allies on your team can have this role, like

Macha is to me, or they can be specific spirits, never met before but solely in charge of guardianship and gatekeeping. This role can be divided into physical and psychic protection among several spirits.
Use this exercise to meet your guardian spirits.

E$_X$ERCI$_S$E 15 – MEETING YOUR SPIRIT GUARDIANS

❶ Do Exercise 1 to reach a meditative state. Do any of the protective exercises you feel drawn to do.

❷ Make an intention to meet you guardians, such as "I ask the God/Goddess/Great Spirit to bring me to my guardians and protectors, to speak together and bond."

❸ Imagine a pathway before you. Follow the path. It leads to your protectors. You see a staircase in the distance. Follow the staircase until you enter a big open space. Your protectors are there.

❹ Introduce yourself to your guardians. You could see them, hear them, or just sense their presence. Several can exist or only one. Ask their names. Ask any questions you have. Ask them how best to invoke their protection. Listen to what they have to say to you through your psychic senses.

❺ When you are finished with this session, follow the stairs to the path, and the path to where you began.

❻ Return your perceptions back to the room. Speak the intention, "I release all that does not serve," three times. This releases any unwanted or harmful energies you may have picked up on your journey.

Use whatever names or methods your guardian spirits give you for invoking their protective powers. The experience will leave you feeling more secure and comfortable with your guardians.

◎ AMULETS ◎

Another useful technique for invoking a daily connection to your guardian spirit allies is to make an amulet of protection. Do Exercise 15 again, but this time, ask your guardians for a symbol of protection for you. Ask for something that connects you to their power. Write it down as soon as you regain normal consciousness before you forget it.

Some symbols are simple, like the standard protection symbols you have seen before, like a cross, Star of David, pentacle, or other charm. Or it could be a symbol unique to your guardians. Pay attention to the pattern and any particular colors. They might not show you specifically, but will tell you that you will see the symbol soon enough. They could even give you a "homework" assignment to research a symbol. Many of the archangels and angelic orders have specific symbols, signs, and sigils to denote their power that can be found in books of magic. They might use Enochian, a magical script, the language of angels. The guardians could tell you to get specific ingredients for the amulet and place them in a bottle or bag.

Once you have the symbol, materials, and information, create an amulet of protection. With intent and thought focused on protection and your guardian, do this when the Moon phase is in the fourth quarter, near the dark New Moon. This is a magical time for protection, since the waning Moon removes unwanted energies and obstacles. Your amulet can be a commercially made piece of jewelry that you bless, charge, and consecrate by tracing its symbol in ritual, or it can be something completely of your own design. I use wooden disks on which I either paint or wood burn. Put your symbol on a piece of paper and keep this amulet in your wallet or purse. As long as you have the intent in it, and the symbol, it will protect you and strengthen the conscious bond to your guardians.

CHAPTER TEN
WORKING IN THE ELEMENTAL WORLD

AS BEINGS LIVING IN THE MATERIAL, physical world, we have material needs. If we focus solely on our spiritual responsibilities, spending hour upon hour in meditation, we lose track of our own needs. It is not selfish to want to be comfortable. In my own spiritual tradition, witchcraft, the ideal is to be balanced. Having too much or too little is unnatural. You need what is right for you. Some spiritual paths disassociate from the material, seeing matter as an illusion. That is true, but some take it to an extreme, in my view. If you are in a body now, you chose to be, and you should enjoy the experience to its fullest. Pay attention to your spiritual needs and your emotions, mind, and body. They all need to be in balance to make a happy, harmonious you.

As we have spiritual allies to help us in our higher aspirations, we have allies responsible for the material world. We all agree to certain rules when we come here to Earth. We obey the laws of gravity, physics, and chemistry. We also obey the laws of karma, Hermetics, astrology, and intention. We are not consciously aware of these rules, but they bind us, and they can work for us. There are spirits responsible for the maintenance of this level of reality. They are the architects and builders who bring things into shape and form. They are the elementals, devas, and nature spirits. These beings can be wonderful allies if you know how to call them.

◎ ELEMENTALS ◎

A misconception plagues the modern mind. In general, people see consciousness as the peak, the end product of matter. We evolve from unconscious one-celled organisms into more and more complex beings. Animals have a distinct consciousness and personality, but they mainly follow their instincts. Only with humankind, and perhaps some would concede ape, dolphin, whale, and elephant, is there sentience, self-awareness, and the ability to reason. Matter developed the mind through millions of years of evolution. That view is a nice way of looking at life, but not the only way.

From a more metaphysical point of view, matter is the peak experience, or end product of consciousness and spirit. The millions of years of evolution were a process to create the perfect physical vehicle for our consciousness. In teachings of Hermes Trismegistus, an ancient teacher who is believed to be the basis of the Greek god Hermes, the Roman Mercury, and the Egyptian Thoth, there is the Principle of Mentalism. This Hermetic law states we are all thoughts in the divine mind. Whatever you call the creator, we are thoughtforms running around in its mind. All matter, energy, time, and consciousness are thoughts, thoughts of the Great Spirit. Everything has a basis in thought and spirit first, then it takes shape until reaching the end result, but there is no end result as the thoughts keep changing, from one to the next. The nature of the universe is extremely intelligent, complex, and ultimately mental.

As creators in our own right, we use the same process, no matter if our creation is a work of art or a piece of machinery. First we have the inspiration for it. The idea comes and we decide to create it. Then we think about how to make it. The idea takes a more concrete form in our minds. Then we start building, giving it actual shape and form. We give it substance. Then we complete it and make it a reality on the material plane.

Fire, Air, Water, Earth

The layers of this creation process are strikingly similar to our symbolism of the four elements. Each one is a layer of our own consciousness and being. Anything taking shape must go through these realms. When we get our inspiration and use our own willpower to set it into motion, we use the element of fire. Fire is the stuff of creation. When we think, we use our air aspect, the mind. The idea changes and takes on the breath of life in our mind. When we give it form, we work in our water aspect. We are working on the astral and emotional levels. True creation does not happen unless the heart and mind are in unison. The astral shape is a template for the physical form. Lastly we give it physical substance. We are working with physical, chemical, and etheric components. We give it true life. This is our earthly aspect.

Each of the four elements has spirits, elementals, governing the creation process. We can call upon them individually, but for a more spectacular and cooperative effort, use them in tandem. The four elements together are powerful forces at work, capable of manifesting anything you need or want. Ritual magicians, witches, shamans, and even some forms of prayer and meditation honor all four directions, honoring the four elements of creation. Here you create a sacred space, a temple. Here you manifest in the material world or remove obstacles.

First, it is wise to connect to each of the four elements and find an ally in each realm. Find a friendly and helpful elemental. Some have different names, others do not. After some journeying, you could even meet those in charge of the realm, the elemental kings and queens.

Everybody has all four elements internally, in the metaphysical sense. We have the fire of our metabolism; fire is also in our spirit. The water is in our blood and organs; we are mostly water held in by flesh. Water is also present in our emotions. Air is the oxygen in our lungs and in our body; it is our mental aspect as well. The trace metals and elements making our bones, organs, and skin are physical manifestations of earth. Everybody has an element or combination of elements that dominate his personality. One may be more practical, earth, and the other emotional, dominated by water. Fiery tempers are obvious, and cool, detached people work in air. Look at your own personality after these exercises and see which elements resonate with you. They indicate traits you need to simply be aware of or balance out.

FIRE

Key Words:	will, light, spirit, power
Gender:	masculine
Direction:	East or South
Colors:	red, orange
Tools:	wand, candle
Angel:	Michael
King:	Notus

Fire is the most nebulous of the four traditional elements. By its very nature, it is closest to the spiritual level. Fire has no physical form like the other elements. It is matter in transition to energy. Fire is the power of action, movement, energy, and intensity. This is the essence of creation.

Fire elementals take the shape of red lizards called salamanders, but other associated animals include foxes, lions, rams, and horses, usually painted in flames. Humanoid beings composed entirely of flame are another form of these elementals.

In human life, fire manifests as strong passion, usually through sexuality or career. Fire people are determined and driven. Those whose Sun sign is in one of the three fire signs, Aries, Leo, or Sagittarius, can probably greatly relate to this passion and intensity.

EₓERCIₛE 16 – MEETING A FIRE ELEMENTAL

❶ Prepare the space for the element of fire by lighting a red or orange candle while thinking of the qualities of fire. If you have a wand, put it next to the candle, creating a small altar or shrine to the element of fire. Use any objects that remind you of fire.

❷ Do Exercise 1 to enter a meditative state. Do any of the protective exercises you feel drawn to do.

❸ Make an intention to travel to the realm of fire and meet an elemental, such as "I ask the God/Goddess/Great Spirit to safely open the doors to the kingdom of fire and draw to me a fire being who is correct and good for me." You can ask for the help of the archangel or traditional king of the element from the Greek tradition.

❹ Stare into the candle flame for a few moments. Close your eyes and visualize the flame before you. With each inhalation imagine the flame getting bigger, until it is the size of a doorway before you.

❺ Visualize yourself stepping through the doorway of flame and into the elemental kingdom of fire. You are sending your own fiery essence and cannot be hurt by this world or those in it. Unlike with physical fire, you will not burn.

❻ There you will be greeted by an elemental. Make contact with it. Ask any questions you have about it or the nature of fire. The elementals are the best guides to explain and show their own element in action.

❼ Thank the elemental and return through the flame doorway, back to this world.

❽ Return your perceptions back to the room. Speak the intention,

"I release all that does not serve," three times. This releases any unwanted or harmful energies from the realm of fire you may have picked up on your journey.

AIR

Key Words:	mind, thought, life
Gender:	masculine
Direction:	South or East
Colors:	yellow, sky blue
Tools:	blade, incense
Angel:	Raphael
King:	Eurius

Air is the province of the mind. Here we express our intellect and ideas. Concepts are explored. Information comes here to be played with, correlated, and related to new forms. Philosophies are given birth. Like the wind, thoughts come and go, floating from one place to the next. They cannot be pinned down. They are free to come and go as they please. Like breath, they enter us in one moment and leave us the next, for a new thought and a new breath.

Air elementals take the shape of winged creatures, including fairylike beings called sylphs. They come as all manner of birds or appear as creatures composed entirely out of invisible air. Gusts of wind reveal their location. The air signs of the zodiac–Gemini, Libra, and Aquarius–are influenced by the rational, logical mind.

EXERCISE 17 – MEETING AN AIR ELEMENTAL

❶ Prepare space for the element of air by lighting a yellow or blue candle while thinking of the qualities of air. You can also light some incense. Lavender is a good air incense. If you have a blade, like a ritual athame or knife, put it next to the candle, creating a small altar or shrine to the element of air. Use any objects that remind you of air.

❷ Do Exercise 1 to enter a meditative state. Do any of the protective exercises you feel drawn to do.

❸ Make an intention to travel to the realm of air and meet an elemental, such as "I ask the God/Goddess/Great Spirit to safely open the doors to the kingdom of air and draw to me an air being who is correct and good for me." You can ask for the help of the archangel or traditional king of the element from the Greek tradition.

❹ Stare into the wisps of incense or visualize smoke clouds if you have no incense. Close your eyes and visualize it swirling into a thick wind, like a tornado. Imagine with each inhalation the cyclone is getting bigger until it is the size of a tunnel before you.

❺ Visualize yourself stepping into the tunnel of wind and into the elemental kingdom of air. You are sending your own airy, mental essence and cannot be hurt by this world or those in it. You will be able to breathe normally.

❻ There you will be greeted by an elemental. Make contact with it. Ask any questions you have about it or the nature of air. The elementals are the best guides to explain and show their own element in action.

❼ Thank the elemental and return through the windy tunnel, back to this world.

❽ Return your perceptions to the room. Speak the intention, "I release all that does not serve," three times. This releases any unwanted or harmful energies from the realm of air you may have picked up on your journey.

WATER

Key Words:	emotion, love, astral
Gender:	feminine
Direction:	West
Colors:	blue, aqua, sea green
Tools:	cup, cauldron, bowl
Angel:	Gabriel
King:	Zephyrus

Water brings us emotion. This kingdom is the realm of healing and regeneration, associated with the underworld, death, and rebirth. West, with the sunset, is the land of endings and many mythologies place paradise just over the western horizon. At its highest form, water is unconditional love, but water rules all manner of loving relationships like romance and family. Water is the medium in which we empathize and relate to others. Water is our compassion, associated with the astral plane, the realm beyond this veil and a step into the invisible spirit world where things take on form before manifesting in the material.

Elementals of this land come in mythological mermaid and mer-man forms, called undines. They appear as animals from the deep, like dolphins, whales, eels, and all types of fish. They even appear in condensed shapes of water or humanoid forms.

In humanity, water is expressed in an emotional nature, leading with the heart. Either you seek to protect the heart or unite it with others. Romantics, mothers, and family archetypes express a watery nature. Cancer, Scorpio, and Pisces are the zodiac water signs.

EXERCISE 18 – MEETING A WATER ELEMENTAL

❶ Prepare the space for the element of water by lighting a blue or green candle while thinking of the qualities of water. Fill a bowl or chalice with water. Create a small altar or shrine to the element. Use any objects that remind you of water.

❷ Do Exercise 1 to enter a meditative state. Do any of the protective exercises you feel drawn to do.

❸ Make an intention to travel to the realm of water and meet an elemental, such as "I ask the God/Goddess/Great Spirit to safely open the doors to the kingdom of water and draw to me a water being who is correct and good for me." You can ask for the help of the archangel or traditional king of the element from the Greek tradition.

❹ Stare into the chalice and catch the light off the candle flame reflected in the water. Close your eyes and visualize the water before you. Imagine it getting bigger in your mind's eye, until the pool of water is the size of the floor before you.

❺ Visualize yourself diving into the water and into the elemental kingdom. You are sending your own emotional, astral essence and cannot be hurt by this world or those in it. You will not drown.

❻ There you will be greeted by an elemental. Make contact with it. Ask any questions you have about it or the nature of water. The elementals are the best guides to explain and show their own element in action.

❼ Thank the elemental and return through the pool, back to this world.

❽ Return your perceptions to the room. Speak the intention, "I release all that does not serve," three times. This releases any unwanted or harmful energies from the realm of water you may have picked up on your journey.

EARTH

Key Words:	physical, material, law
Gender:	feminine
Direction:	North
Colors:	green, black, brown
Tools:	stone, salt, pentacle, coin
Angel:	Uriel
King:	Boreas

Earth is the densest of the four elements and the easiest to understand. Earth is more physical and less symbolic than the other three. Soil, rocks, sand, metals, and chemical elements are earth. Our bodies are made of it and the land as well. Earth translates in our life to our material nature. The food we eat, our clothes, homes, money, and other material concerns are of the earth plane.

Earth elementals express themselves through the wee folk of myth. They are the little people like gnomes, dwarves, and some would say elves and fairies, but I think the fairies fall closer to general nature spirits. They express themselves through earthy animals, including stags, deer, bears, snakes, bulls, cows, and goats. They appear as people made of soil or stone.

Humans highly influenced by the element of earth are practical, cautious, prepared, stable, and hard workers. They let their practicality rule rather than their emotions, mind, or will. Taurus, Virgo, and Capricorn are the three zodiac earth signs.

EXERCISE 19 – MEETING AN EARTH ELEMENTAL

❶ Prepare space for the element of earth by lighting a green, black, or brown candle while thinking of the qualities of earth. Create a small altar or shrine to the element of earth by putting a stone, crystal, or bowl of soil near the candle. Use any other objects that remind you of earth.

❷ Do Exercise 1 to enter a meditative state. Do any of the protective exercises you feel drawn to do.

❸ Make an intention to travel to the realm of earth and meet an elemental, such as "I ask the God/Goddess/Great Spirit to safely open the doors to the kingdom of earth and draw to me an earth being who is correct and good for me." You can ask for the help of the archangel or traditional king of the element from the Greek tradition.

❹ Close your eyes and visualize a dark cave before you. The cave leads to the realm of earth and your elemental ally.

❺ Visualize yourself walking into the cave and into the elemental kingdom. You are sending your own etheric essence and cannot be hurt by this world or those in it. This elemental kingdom is like an etheric shadow to the material world.

❻ There you will be greeted by an elemental. Make contact with it. Ask any questions you have about it or the nature of earth. The elementals are the best guides to explain and show their own element in action.

❼ Thank the elemental and return through the tunnel, back to this world.

❽ Return your perceptions to the room. Speak the intention, "I release all that does not serve," three times. This releases any unwanted or harmful energies from the realm of earth you may have picked up on your journey.

◎ THE MAGIC CIRCLE ◎

Now that you have connected to each of the four elemental worlds you can call on these spirit allies to manifest your needs and desires.

Causing change in accord with your own needs is magic. Other traditions call it prayer or manifestation.

Magic has been maligned by many. They fear magic because
they fear being controlled or manipulated. Magic, and any energy
in general, is not evil if you do not use it with evil intent. Intent is
the ruler of magic. Once you understand magic, you know you cannot be manipulated or controlled if you do not want to be. You
have the defenses. There is no white magic or black magic, just
people using magic for helping or harming, and there is no harm in
helping yourself.

As cocreators in our universe, we are already using our intentions to shape our reality, consciously or unconsciously. Would it
not be better to use them in a conscious, directed way with powerful results? We would be more responsible and aware of our
energies and actions. These are the principles of this universe we
are using all the time. Understand them. We are here to master this
level of reality and incarnation. Magic and psychic abilities are tools
to help us, and everybody has them at their fingertips, just like the
spiritual support team. Call our guides and guardians during ritual.
Our allies in spirit are magical allies too.

The magic circle is a simple ritual that can be adapted to anyone's faith. The basic structure comes from Western ritual magic,
but it is only one technique. The circle itself requires no set of
beliefs other than a belief in energy and sacredness and an intent to
change your reality. The structure involves the four elements, honoring them, bringing them together in sacred space, and sending
your intention out to manifest. You call the four elements together
and then read your intention. While reading, visualize your intent
occurring and raise this energy up with your arms to go out into the
universe. This is called raising the cone of power. Then the remaining energy is grounded by touching the floor and visualizing it going
into the earth. Send the intention of Earth healing with it.

Your formed intention is considered a spell. Write out what you
want to happen in the form of a petition. Ask the higher divine
powers you work with for their aid. You can call on any other spirit

allies you wish to help, including angels, pagan gods, Christian saints, power animals, or spirit guides. Here is an example.

> I, [state your name here], ask in the name of the
> God/Goddess/Great Spirit to be granted
>
> _____,
>
> in a way that is for my highest good, harming none. So be it.

Witches usually end spells with "So mote it be." It means the same as "so be it."

If I personally were doing a spell for love, I may call in Venus, the goddess of love. If I needed to be purified and transformed, I might ask St. Germain to join me with his cleansing violet flame. In general, it is more helpful to do magic to gain things and bring things toward you with the waxing Moon and do magic to remove obstacles or illness on the waning Moon. Check an astrological calendar or almanac for that information.

Write out your intentions clearly and ask for exactly what you want. Be as specific as possible. Traditionally, you can do up to three intentions per ceremony and one circle per day. Finding out your material needs is a great insight to the spiritual road you travel.

Prepare with ritual tools. A wand or blade can be used to mark the boundaries of the circle, tracing it in the air. Intent works just as well if you shy away from ritual tools. Use your finger instead. Four elemental candles, set in each of the four directions can be lit when you call on the elements. Spell papers are usually burned or buried afterward. If you burn them, make sure you have a flame-proof cauldron or container to keep the fire. Incense, oils, and crystals can be set upon your altar. An altar does not mean you are putting some object before your belief in divinity. This is not idol worship. You are not worshiping your tools. An altar is simply a magical workspace (see figure 9 on page 148).

Learn the basic steps to the magic circle ritual as outlined in Exercise 20, then modify it to fit your own needs and traditions.

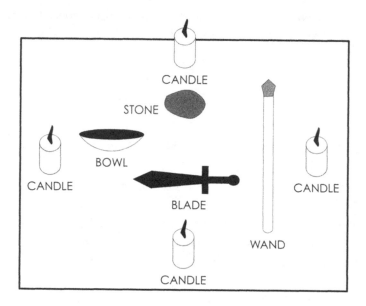

Figure 9. Altar

Before starting, make sure you know where the four compass directions are relative to your altar. Then decide whom you will be calling for each element. You can call a specific elemental you met in
your previous meditation. Archangels and elemental kings are popular. Try totem animals, deities, or ascended masters. There are
many options available to you.

Exercise 20 – Casting the Magic Circle

❶ Prepare the space by setting up your altar and getting out any
ritual tools that would make you feel comfortable.

❷ Do Exercise 1 to enter a meditative state. Do any of the protective exercises you feel drawn to do.

❸ As in Exercise 10, visualize a circle of light around you, perfect
in shape or form. Starting in the North, trace a clockwise circle

with the edge of your wand or blade or the tip of your finger. Cast the ring three times, saying, "I cast this circle to protect us from all forces, positive, negative, or otherwise that may come to do us harm. I ask that only those who come for our highest good enter this circle. I create a sacred space between the worlds where our will creates our reality." I ask for "all spirits who come only in perfect love and trust, completely correct for my intentions."

❹ Facing North, call to the element of earth and any beings who embody the element of earth for you. For example, I would call the element of earth and the stag. Then light your earth candle.

❺ Facing East, call to the element of fire and any beings who embody the element of fire for you. I might call the element of fire and the fox. Light your fire candle.

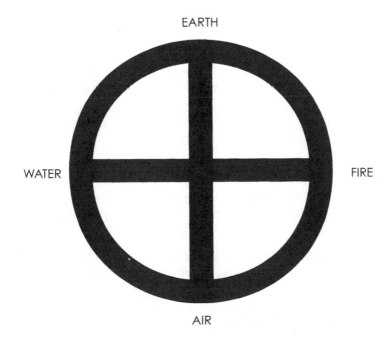

Figure 10. Magic Circle

⑥ Facing South, call to the element of air and any beings who embody the element of air for you. I usually call on the element of air and the crow. Light your air candle and incense.

⑦ Facing West, call to the element of water and any beings who embody the element of water for you. Following the animal pattern, I would call the dolphin. Light the water candle and you may even drink from your bowl or chalice.

⑧ Call on your allies to be with you, including the Great Spirit or any emissary of divine love. In this example, I would call the Celtic goddess Danu and the god Dagda. Someone from a Christian background could call on Jesus and Mary. For those with Egyptian spiritual beliefs, Osiris and Isis work well.

⑨ Visualize yourself at the center of the circle, with the arms of a cross of light going through your heart, out to the four directions. You embody the center, the divine spirit through which the four elements will work. The circle might shift into a sphere.

⑩ Read or speak your intention spell. Visualize the outcome. If you choose, burn it and toss the paper into the flameproof container, like a cauldron. Raise your arms projecting the energy out of the top of the circle, still visualizing your goal.

⑪ Lower your arms across your heart, like an Egyptian pharaoh, still focusing on your goal. Release the intention out to the universe. Let the elements manifest for you. Forget about the intention until it manifests. Know the universe will provide.

⑫ Touch the floor, grounding any remaining energies into the earth. Feel any free-floating energy go into the ground.

⑬ Starting in the North and moving counterclockwise West, South, then East, thank and release the element and all beings called on from that direction.

⓮ Thank all other divine beings you have asked to help you.

⓯ Trace the outline of the circle, counterclockwise starting at North, saying, "I release this circle to do its work. The circle is undone but not broken." I visualize the circle expanding out like a drop in a pool of water, creating ripples across the universe.

In essence, that is the magic circle. You can add more to it, including music, chanting, food, wine, more tools, and elaborate ritual. Research your own beliefs and traditions to make this sacred space and time yours. Ceremony is a wonderful and powerful tool.

◎ DEVAS, NATURE SPIRITS, AND THE MATERIAL WORLD ◎

Now that you have made friends with the four elements, work on your relationship with the devas and nature spirits. How do the devas and nature spirits differ from the elementals or even each other? Some say they do not and that the breakdown is only semantics. But in my mind there is a distinction and so I deal with them a little differently.

Devas and nature spirits are more responsible than elementals for the physical, material world, including the plants, animals, and general balance of the environment. For many, they sound like an earth elemental. Earth elementals involve physicality in general. The devas get more specific. Although humans are made of all the elements, we are not elementals ourselves. The devas and nature spirits are particularly tuned in with the elementals that reflect their nature–for plants it would be earth, for volcanoes, fire, etc. Likewise They are made of the elemental material and, as a nonhumanoid consciousness, appear much closer to the elementals, but they are not elementals in the strictest sense. Devas and nature spirits are called on only where they are relevant. If you were doing magic to clean an environmental disaster, you can call on the devas and nature spirits of that area to help you and ideally to ask their permission first.

The devas are the architects. They create patterns; they hold the forms or blueprints. There is a deva for almost anything–dandelions, amethyst, seashells, pine trees, and probably even computer microchips. Computers have form and have probably attracted a devic intelligence to guide them. The chief deva is called the overlighting deva because it coordinates the other devas in its order. The deva of a particular dandelion is like the child of the overlighting deva of dandelions. The overlighting deva is responsible for all dandelions everywhere. People sometimes call devas overlighting angels and angelic orders. I like the thought of nature angels, but devas differ from the typical winged concept of angels held by so many people. In the Hindu tradition, the word *deva* often translates into "god."

The nature spirits are the material consciousness of different substances. They fill out the patterns created by the devas and make them physical. Nature spirits are most likely elementals who choose to master more than one element. They bring a synthesis of the elements together. As they master more complex forms, some theorize they become different beings, including angels, dragons, and human souls.

A forest has one general overlighting deva responsible for the forest as a whole. Inside the forest are devas and nature spirits for all the different plants and animal types. At the same time this forest deva is working with the overlighting devas responsible for each species of tree, plant, animal, and insect in the forest. The web of nature is complex.

There is an overlighting deva of quartz crystals, holding the six-sided crystal pattern. An individual deva oversees the new crystal bed growing in the earth. The energy and consciousness of the supersaturated silicon dioxide solution is the nature spirit. As the solution cools, it grows into the pattern of quartz. Without the devic influence, it dries too quickly and never grows into the crystal.

When working with a deva or nature spirit system, you need only call on the overlighting deva of the area. For nature spirits, Pan, the Greek satyr god of the forest and woods, is the global nature spirit called on to direct the appropriate beings in ritual, healing, or magic. Many equate Pan with the Celtic horned god Cernunnos, but in my experience, they are two different beings with similar attributes. I was told Cernunnos is like the big brother of Pan and carries a similar function in other, less physical realms connected to ours, but for earthly nature spirits, we should call on Pan.

Communication with devas and nature spirits is fairly simple. You need to be near them physically. If you want to commune with the devas and nature spirits of the forest, sit in the forest. Be around those with whom you want to communicate. Immerse yourself in their environment. Living in houses, walking on concrete, we are very disconnected from the natural world and have to consciously act to reconnect to it. For the purpose of communication, it is diffi-cult to distinguish devas and nature spirit unless you ask. They can have an entirely different answer for you than the information in this book. As always, follow what is right for you. Different people need and hear information in different ways.

E x E R C I s E 21 – SPEAKING WITH DEVAS

❶ Choose a space for your devic and nature spirit connection. Forests are great, but backyards and parks do well too. You can do this with a single tree, flower, or stone.

❷ Do Exercise 1 to get into a receptive state. Do any of the pro-tective exercises you feel drawn to do.

❸ Ask to speak to the overlighting deva or devas of this realm. Ask to connect to the nature spirits.

❹ Wait and listen. If you do not hear anything, ask again and introduce yourself. It can take time to connect, but for most, the voices come with surprising ease.

❺ If you hear many voices at once, ask them to speak one at a time. Common experience is that the beings have been waiting for you to notice or take the time to talk with them. Listen to what they say and ask them any questions. (Note: Any medicinal or herbal advice given by a spirit should be thoroughly checked out with a qualified medical professional or herbalist.)

❻ Thank the spirit allies who are with you now. Bid them farewell and return to your normal waking consciousness.

◎ SPIRITUAL HEALING AND THE BODY DEVA ◎

Since there is a deva for everything, each one of us constantly and unconsciously works with several devas. We each have a deva of our body, and there is an overlighting being for the healing of the physical body. All the material that forms the patterns of our external body and internal organs is alive and conscious. We can talk to our body. If illness is the body's way of getting attention, we should give it attention and find out what is wrong. Each illness and disease is a manifestation of specific problems. Those with heart problems are working on issues with love. Those with throat problems, on communication. Disease affecting the reproductive system deals with sexuality, guilt, and shame. Colon problems often denote problems with power. An excellent reference on energy anatomy and disease correspondence is Caroline Myss's *Anatomy of the Spirit.*

By connecting with these forces, our own body, we can find out our problems more clearly, ask what to do to fix them, and seek the aid of these bodily allies to help heal. Once they know you know the problem and you are taking steps to fix it, the body starts working with your conscious intentions. If you only pay it meditative lip service and do not follow through, you will not heal. You cannot fool your own inherent body wisdom.

After getting laid off from a job, I had my annual scheduled physical. A liver enzyme test came back high. The doctor tested me for all forms of hepatitis. All tests were negative. The doctor then suggested that I go three months without any alcohol to see if my liver was only over active. I do not drink much to begin with, but he wanted to make sure. The test result was still high. I finally did a meditation to connect to my liver and figure out what the problem was. My liver said three words to me, "fear and anger." "What does that mean?" I wondered. I did not know, but I thought I should take care of it.

I learned that according to Chinese medicine the liver gets blocked when you are repressing anger. The more I thought about it, the more I identified with this information. I started working with a flower essence consultant on this issue. Flower essences are energy medicine based on the energy signature of the flower in cooperation with the flower's consciousness, its deva, and its nature spirits. Each energy signature works with particular emotions in the human body.

The first healing crisis was dealing healthily with anger. I thought anger should be suppressed in order to be a spiritual, loving person. Anger is a defense mechanism, often protecting you from others who would take advantage of you. There are healthy and unhealthy channels for it. I chose not to channel it at all. Other flower essences were used for fear issues and trusting the universe.

After working with the flower essences for a while, I went back to the doctor, had the liver test again, and it was normal. The doctor concluded I had lost some weight and the previously high test results were due to fatty acid buildup in the liver. That might even be true in the medical sense, but I know my truth and listening to my body helped me deal with it.

EₓERCIₛE 22 –
COMMUNICATING WITH YOUR BODY DEVA

❶ Do Exercise 1 to get into a receptive state. Do any of the protective exercises you feel drawn to do. I suggest you lie down and get comfortable. If you have a specific place on the body to speak to, like the liver, touch it and gently massage it.

❷ Ask to be connected to your body deva and the nature spirits comprising your body.

❸ Focusing on a specific place, feel your perception and consciousness travel to that part of the body. If you are connecting to the liver, feel as if you are inside, looking out of the liver. If you are connecting to the heart, feel as if you are looking out of the heart and rib cage. If you are in good health, expand your awareness to the entire body, from every hair on your head down to the tips of your toes. Use your imagination.

❹ Speak to the specific organ, body system, or your entire body. Ask if it has any problems or any needs for you. Listen without judgment. Ask what you can do to help it and restore balance.

❺ Thank your body and your deva, return to normal waking consciousness, and make any necessary changes in your life.

This check-in exercise is great occasionally, even when you are feeling in top health. Sometimes you head things off at the pass before they manifest in your physical body.

Healing Work with Clients

If you do any kind of healing work, guided visualization, pranic healing, Reiki, or polarity therapy, invoke the Overlighting Deva of the Human Body to be with you. The Overlighting Deva of

Healing is very helpful as well. Spiritual healing in its many forms is working through things that block health. We use energy and intention in various forms to effect the healing. You can guide your clients through Exercise 23 to find their own issues. You can work in cooperation with a client's own energy body. If the client cannot hear the message, you could translate for her. As healers we have to be careful we send the true message and do not let our egos get in the way. The client then must determine if the advice is right for her.

As a metaphysical healer, if you are not licensed to make diagnosis, refrain from doing so, even if you are certain of the problem. Offer advice, suggestions, and your own intuition about the problem, and let your clients seek medical care in conjunction with your therapy. This can save you from serious legal problems in the future.

Shamanic Concepts of Illness

Mystical cultures attribute illness to many things. In Central and South American tribal cultures, if you offend your spirit animal and it leaves you, the forces of illness and bad luck easily work against you. Sickness spirits enter your body and bring illness. You need to regain your power animal to guard you and chase out the sickness, or you need a shaman, a doctor of the spirit, to get you a new animal protector and help remove the offending sickness spirits.

Modern medical practitioners would translate these sickness spirits into the physical world of viruses and bacteria. If these illnesses were strictly physical, however, the shaman would have little luck curing them. The virus or bacteria can be the physical agent of sickness, but sickness has a spiritual root. As the illness is related to our own blocks to health and well-being, we create or attract our own energy blocks to literally cut us off from good health. They can be removed with shamanistic healing techniques, along with the whole range of holistic health therapies and energy medicines.

Implants

The new, in vogue name for these blocks in the New Age community is *implants*. The word, although quite accurate, conjures up images of little creatures placing microchips in us. Though I do not doubt that many people may have experienced this, I am talking about spiritual implants and limitation devices. The word *implant* obviously suggests someone or something has placed something into you and the results are not your fault. Some blocks are self-created, some are attracted, and some are implanted by other beings, but they are your responsibility to clear now. Understand why this happened to you on a spiritual level and release it. Most blocks to our health are self-created thoughtforms.

Often you will have a spirit ally whose specialty is clearing away blocks to health. I think everybody has one or can request one. We each work with guides who are healers. If we are consciously unaware of them, they come while we sleep and dream. If you work in the tribal sickness paradigm, your guide is a power animal or ancient shamanic guide. If you feel you have implants or blocks, help may come in the form of a psychic surgeon. If you simply believe the cause is blocked emotions or an unhealthy attitude, your healer spirit can be as simple, giving you dreams where she lays hands on you or guides you to the correct doctor, counselor, dietician, or gym to help you with your health issues. Look for the simple solutions first. They work best.

Create a special ceremony in sacred space to connect with this guide. These spaces are sometimes called healing chambers or coning sessions. I do a magic circle ritual, since balance of the four elements is essential to health. Basically, you are creating a sacred space through spoken intent, visualization, or ceremony. Speak about the problem you are working on in your health. The issue can be physical or in the emotional and mental realms. Ask for guidance and healing. You can feel the guides "working" on you through subtle and not so subtle sensations in your body. I feel my allies working on me even outside of a healing ritual, as when I go to a flower essence session. I invoke them to aid my consultant in picking the best essences for me. Then I start to feel light-headed.

◎ MANIFESTATION ◎

If there is a deva responsible for our physical body, then there is a deva for our material needs. This spirit probably helps out in our magical work and circle rituals even though we do not specifically call on it. That is why I ask for "all spirits who come in perfect love and trust, completely correct for my intentions." Those few words open the doors to a whole host of benign spirits I am not consciously aware of. You can call this ally your manifestation deva, prosperity deva, or most popularly, your money deva.

This is another form of a material spirit, helping us get by in the material world. If in previous lives we have had no experience with money or business, this ally can be a vital necessity to our support team. Others who are very fortunate have learned the lessons of abundance consciousness and prosperity from these allies and apply them to daily living, keeping their allies happy, even if they are consciously unaware of them. Ask your allies the secrets of abundance. A general rule is you need to give to make room to receive. Your own generosity will return to you. Your allies will, of course, have specific information only for you.

Money devas help build the networks in which we acquire the coin of the realm. They did not always work this way. When barter was the main form of commerce, devas helped us trade and find others who needed what we had and had what we needed. When we were a hunter/gatherer society, they led us to game or berries. Now most of the world uses slips of paper and disks of metal to stand for something valuable. Devas help us acquire those too. The modern money deva has gone through many changes.

Our relationship to our money deva is in effect our relationship with our own prosperity. It can be a spirit ally, but until we make friends with it, a money deva appears to be a hindrance. When doing a meditation to meet the money deva, people have visions where they are choking, hitting, or stepping on it. That represents their relationship with money.

An acquaintance of mine went to a workshop called "Meeting Your Money Deva." There he discovered a prosperity spirit ally shaped like a giant insect. In his inner vision, he saw himself choking the insect. By making friends with it instead, his prosperity increased. Every time he sees that type of insect in physical form, he knows to check his own blocks to prosperity at the time. He might be missing a golden opportunity, and the money deva reminds him.

To effectively work with this ally, we need to take a look at how we think about money. Do you see it as an acceptable standard and believe that you should get paid well for your work? Do you feel money is the root of all evil? These are not either/or questions. You can feel both. We have a lot of conflicting thoughts about money that prevent us from being comfortable. Most people are locked into a poverty consciousness and a mind-set where there is scarcity, hoarding resources. If you are prosperous, you know you must give away and release some of what you have. That opens space for you to receive more. If you stop the flow, you stop receiving too.

Working with a money deva helps show us our blocks if we have any. Then we consciously work toward a more prosperous life. Prosperity consciousness is not only about money, so perhaps calling this being a money deva is a severe faux pas, but money is the part of prosperity people easily relate to. Prosperity comes in comfort, time, friendship, love, success, satisfaction, and happiness. Think about your relationship to those qualities.

EXERCISE 23 –
MEETING YOUR PROSPERITY DEVA

❶ Do Exercise 1 to get into a receptive state. Do any of the protective exercises you feel drawn to do.

❷ Ask to be connected to and communicate with your prosperity deva in a manner for your highest good.

❸ Visualize a doorway of light opening up before you. As the portal opens, your prosperity spirit ally comes through. It can be in any shape you can imagine, animal, vegetable, mineral, humanoid, or formless. Let the shape come to you. It could be connected to one of your other spirit allies, or your other spirit allies could play intermediary between you and your prosperity ally.

❹ Speak to your deva of prosperity. Do you have any indications of your relationship to it? Ask if it has any problems or any needs of you. Ask it what kind of relationship you have with it and how it can be better. Listen without judgment.

❺ Thank your deva, return to normal waking consciousness, and make any necessary changes in your life.

Whenever you are reminded of the shape and form of the deva, then you need to speak with it and look at your money concerns. For example, if your money deva looks like a rabbit, every time you see a rabbit and think of your deva, it is a sign to look inward about your financial situation, unless you spend your days at a rabbit farm.

◎ CRYSTAL, PLANT, AND FAIRY SPIRITS ◎

Nature spirits are the consciousness of the living things around you, plants, trees, rocks, crystals, and metals. Each has a form of consciousness. You can speak to the communal consciousness of the forest or the individual beings within the forest. You can speak to the archetype of the beetle or the beetle crawling on the tree next to you. It is all a matter of viewpoint.

Anything you think of as a tool is really an ally. Your home, car, and computer have a certain measure of consciousness. They are made from wood, metal, and crystal, built with an intent. If you do crystal healing, you see crystals as equipment at first. The same thing with an herbalist–you equate your relationship with dande-lion root to a surgeon's relationship with his scalpel.

If you deepen your spirit experience with these "tools," you will discover they are allies. They are your partners who want to successfully do the work. They have greater insight into the prob-lems than you do. They are alive. Any of the metaphysical healing disciplines eventually lead to this experience, while the surgeon would never consider his scalpel as his ally. His field does not encourage the psychic and spiritual experiences to understand this. Most surgeons think their skill is what heals. Skill is neces-sary, but a good surgeon is an instrument for healing, through which the higher powers work. We are all instruments and we are all allies.

Charging

Whenever using a crystal or herb, place an intent into it. In magic, this is called charging your tools. Through a spiritual connection to our tools through our psychic talents, we can catalyze the healing actions of many substances. The natural power of a substance is activated. Think of it as turning on the light switch. Herbs and crys-tals are much more powerful when catalyzed.

A charged immune system tincture is much more powerful than a mass-produced one. It carries a bit of personal energy and intent into it. Even a tincture from a qualified herbalist is stronger if made by one who adds his or her intent and has an intimate connection with the plant world. I am not an experienced herbalist, but a tinc-ture I made to fight colds using echinacea and goldenseal tends to work in one or two doses, compared to others my family has bought in a pharmacy, requiring many doses.

Exercise 24 – CHARGING A CRYSTAL OR HERB

❶ Do Exercise 1 to get into a receptive state. Do any of the protective exercises you feel drawn to do.

❷ Ask to be connected to the substance you are holding. Visualize your perspective, your vision, traveling down your arms until you are inside the substance.

❸ Tell the substance you would like to work with it. Ask permission and wait for a response. You can visualize how you are going to use it, like mixing it into a remedy, making it into a charm, or using it in a healing session.

❹ If you get a positive response, ask to cleanse the substance of unwanted or harmful energies. Visualize white or violet light consuming the item, burning away unwanted energy. If it is a crystal, blow away any unwanted energy using your breath.

❺ Charge the substance to work in harmony with the will of the God/Goddess/Great Spirit, for the highest good of all involved. If you have a specific intention, like healing, improving memory, or bringing prosperity, place it in the substance now.

❻ Ask that only those who are in harmony with the highest good can change this intention.

❼ Thank the substance and return to normal waking consciousness. Use the item as intended.

Fairies

Fairies are the last catchall category of nature spirits. Most people feel they are the same as the elementals, devas, and nature spirits. They are the embodiment of the land and plants. They live in a higher realm as caretakers of the land, the Land of Faery. Other legends say they are the fallen and defeated pagan gods of old, particularly the old gods of the British Isles, who now live under the hills as the wee people. They maintain their pacts for those of the old ways who still remember them, and they appear as fairies, brownies, leprechauns, and elves. They love those who treat them kindly and with respect and play horrible jokes on those who ignore or insult them. Modern witches keep the pacts of the old ways. Shamanistic journeys often reveal their presence in the underworld. They can be reached through journeys, dreams, and the psychic sight. I have a covenmate who works with fairies extensively and would probably make a good argument they are something else entirely. Fairy spirit guides are increasingly common. They are very playful. By their nature, fairies are an elusive bunch, and what is a fairy to one, may not be to another. My advice: find one and ask it, nicely. Respect is the watchword of fairy work.

Spirit allies are found everywhere, not only in the spirit worlds. Help does not come only from above, but also from below and next to us. Helpful allies are all around us, right beside us, and even inside us. Take a good look around.

CHAPTER ELEVEN

BUILDING A BETTER SPIRIT

WE ARE CREATOR GODS. THE SAME ability used to create us from the Great Spirit is an inherent power in all of us. We create every second of the day and are not even aware of it. Our bodies break down the chemicals we put into them and create the substances we need, through digestion, metabolism, and breathing. We continually re-create all our organs every seven years. Every thought or image we have of something, we create. We do not manifest these all physically, but we create them on some level. Anything can be created. Accept no limits, as long as it does not infringe on the free will of others.

Some people are more focused on the abstract creation process than others. They become the artists, painters, writers, but they live in a smaller, personal world of creation. Others do not know they create, but have a larger arena. They are the politicians, spiritual leaders, cult personalities, entertainment moguls, and industry executives. These people have the resources to get others to work on their creations.

As creator gods, and that is gods with a small g, we build so many creations unconsciously we are cluttering up the astral worlds. Working with spirit is working with energy, and now that we have some background in energy work, we need to be more responsible for our creations. We need to be responsible for our thoughts. I used to think this was akin to the thought police, or karma police, having a little voice telling me not to think such things. We have to actively work to watch our thoughts and actions. Thoughts are more difficult to stop because they are so much more spontaneous than actions. It is hard not to think bad things when you are upset, angry, or frightened. As human beings, we all have our moments in the dark, but thoughts are as much an engine to create reality as actions.

◎ NEUTRALIZATION ◎

The first step is to take responsibility for harmful creations set in motion as we make them. The key is neutralization and intent. I used to worry a lot. My vivid imagination expected the worst. If someone was late meeting me, I would assume she was in an accident. I never jumped to the logical conclusion of traffic, starting late, or even forgetting the appointment; I started at the most horrific conclusion and would paint the scene in my mind in great detail. If I do that now, I say to myself or out loud, "I neutralize that thought." In my mind's eye, I will paint a big white X over the image, or visualize it being stamped CANCELLED or NEUTRAL-IZED in white letters.

I learned neutralization in witchcraft classes, but later found out that many people use the technique, including lightworkers, Reiki masters, and shamanic healers. If you do not send out the intent to neutralize it, the energy you created can become a thoughtform with the original harmful intention, and manifest. We are all guardians of this reality, responsible for what we create. If the person you accidentally, or purposely, send this energy to is not able to protect himself, then the event could occur. Even if you do not think to neutralize it right away, but later reflect on your actions, neutralize it anyway. Intent can move beyond time. Be responsible.

As you continue this practice, and for a while every other phrase out of your mouth may be "I neutralize that," you start to automatically program yourself into a new way of thinking. You will not say harmful things as often.

◎ COMPLEX CONSTRUCTS ◎

Once you take responsibility for your own creations and thought-forms, you can use the ability to benefit yourself and others. You can construct a spirit form, an ally of sorts, to perform a certain function. You are making an energy tool out of preexisting energies, mostly your own personal energy and willpower. Some ambient energy around you becomes part of the mix. Constructs are a great way to keep intents going while freeing yourself to do other things.

Three main parts exist in creating a semipermanent construct. The first is the actual building. Building can be done in the magic circle, but does not have to be. Through any combination of intent, ritual, visualization, spoken word, and energy manipulation, you create the construct, much like an intention or spell.

Select a Goal

Decide on a goal. Any effect you want to maintain for a period of time can be your goal. Wards, or protection constructs, are most popular. They take form as a construct around your home pro-grammed to protect you, your family, and valuables from danger. Wards can be modified in many ways. For magical stores, they have the intent to stop shoplifters. In business they bring prosperity, guiding the right people into the store and encouraging them to spend money. An art studio can have a creativity spirit construct, something to inspire and refresh. Body workers and healers can have a construct of safety, comfort, and healing. The limits are only your imagination and willpower.

Construct a Thoughtform

Once you have a goal, decide how to construct a thoughtform that will maintain the goal. What visuals will you need? For protection magic, visualize a ring of light around the area, a crystal sphere of protection, an energy pyramid, a castle wall, or maze to confuse and neutralize harm. To prevent shoplifting, imagine your own security device, an energy screen over all the exits, preventing unpaid items from leaving. To increase sales, imagine little mouths or faces on the walls psychically acting as salespeople, pointing out all the good items you have. You are not forcing others to buy, merely advertising. Everything is done in a spirit of correctness and harming none.

Write out the instructions of the construct, as specifically as needed. Ask it to protect you from all harm, warn you of harm that it cannot protect you from, make your home invisible to burglars, prevent all thefts, find lost objects, boost your creative powers when called on, or create a space conducive to psychic reading and healings. Imagine you are leaving a memo for someone who works for you while you go on vacation. Make the instructions as clear, concise, and short as possible to prevent confusion.

Create a Ritual

Now design a ritual using these pieces. I have more luck inside a magic circle since it will contain all the energy until I finish construction, but other techniques are also successful. Add elements to the ritual that suit you. If doing a protection construct, you can charge some salt water in conjunction with creating the construct. Then anoint your windows and doors with the water. Sprinkle it around the perimeter of your yard. Incense serves the same function.

Bind the Energies

Next bind the energies together so the construct stays as a unit. Naming the construct helps. A name gives the energy a sense of identity. When you call to it, you both know the relationship. Some sort of vessel for the spirit form also serves to bind it. Spells on specific places like houses or buildings can be bound to the actual building as the vessel. For more unusual tasks not bound to a specific location, use a crystal as the home and vessel for the construct when not in use. If the construct is continually in use and not bound to a location, make a talisman. Create a symbol to represent it, and use that symbol when invoking the construct. Carry a charm, medallion, or piece of paper with the symbol on it, so the construct works with you. Draw it in the air with your fingers to activate it.

Maintain the Construct

Once the spirit construct is created and bound together with its name, function, and vessel, you must feed it. Proper care and feeding is an important part of its health and well-being. Feeding means giving the construct more energy through thought, recognition, credit, and visualization. If you make it and completely forget about it, the construct will be worn away by the astral winds. The machine simply erodes with the spiritual equivalent of rust before crumbling away, or it will seek a new source of food and try to leave. If you maintain it, it can last indefinitely. Every so often, repeat the visualizations that created it. Draw its symbol to reactivate the programs. Hold the vessel when thinking about it. When it works, thank it. Acknowledge the construct for all its work. These actions put more of your personal energy into it, making the spirit stronger. If you thank your prosperity construct in your store for every day's sales, then it will work harder to continue the praise. If you cease to praise the construct and forget about it, it fades away. Constructs want to hold on to the essence they have and fulfill the purpose given to them.

When you are no longer in need of the construct, you have two choices. One is to disassemble it. The other is to set it free. Almost all constructs do not have enough awareness to exist on their own. They exist, but freedom would be like throwing a hammer in the woods when you no longer need it. The hammer exists in the woods, and will eventually break down, but someone may stumble upon it and hurt himself. Alternately they could pick the hammer up and use it as a construction tool or as a weapon. A construct is a tool with no discernment on its own. So when you move, disassemble a construct if the energy is tied to your house. If you like it and want to keep the construct, put it in another vessel to take with you and set up in your new home. If you no longer need it at all, by disassembling it, you set the energy free to go on another journey.

Quite rarely you will find a spirit construct that takes on its own life. It grows into self-awareness and becomes different from the typical construct. Creating constructs is an art. Some, like paintings, music, or any art form, take on a life of their own. In these cases, instead of dismantling it, you can ask the spirit form if it wants to be free. Ask it what it would need of you to do this. Visualize the connection between it and its vessel or location being severed. This should be done only if the spirit feels benevolent. If the life it has acquired seems harmful or mired, you should consider dismantling it. This is an act of love and release, along with protection for others. When in doubt, offer to send it to the light of God/Goddess/Great Spirit to do what is best. Ask your other spirit allies for help and advice.

◎ HOME PROTECTION SPIRITS ◎

The first construct to make is one for home protection. Homes have their own consciousness about them. They absorb the energies around them from the people who live in them. Home protection constructs are fairly easy to make because they have so much of this naturally stored ambient energy connecting you to it.

If the home has had a lot of unhappiness, abuse, or other things that can leave an unwanted imprint in the home's energy, you will have to do a clearing. Burn purifying incense. Visualize white or violet light clearing the place. Use rose water in misting bottles. With every technique, put out the intention you want to clear the space of harmful energy.

Once the home is clear, follow Exercise 25 to create a home protection construct. You will need a bowl of sea salt and any material you use to create a magic circle. Write out what you want the construct to do. Use this example or change it to suit your personal needs:

> I, [state your name here[, ask in the name of the
> God/Goddess/Great Spirit to create a spirit of protection
> around my home in a way that is for my highest good,
> harming none. So be it.

EXERCISE 25 – HOME PROTECTION CONSTRUCT

❶ Cast a magic circle, as in Exercise 20.

❷ In the circle, hold the bowl of sea salt and charge it like you would a crystal or herb, as in Exercise 24. Charge it with the intention of protection.

❸ Start visualizing any protection images that come to you around your home. Visualize a pyramid of light around your house. I often use the image of an octahedron, one pyramid on top of another, one upside down, both joined at the bases. The octahedron looks like an eight-sided diamond. This way the home is protected as much from below as above. If you are in an apartment, the image can cut though other apartments, but will protect only yours unless you visualize it over the entire building.

❹ Name your construct if you so choose. The name can be as simple as the street or building name. Choose something you will not forget.

❺ Invite any other spirit allies or guardians to aid in the construction of this form or to protect your home. Dragon and wolf spirits often seek you out to aid in protection, guarding from the roof or astrally wrapping themselves around the building. They are not part of your construct, but an addition to it, unless you purposely shape your construct into the form of an animal and give it instructions to behave as such.

⑥ Read your intention, burn it, and raise the cone of power like you would in a circle ritual. Ground the energy. Release the circle.

⑦ If you have a yard, spread the salt in a clockwise circle from the North all the way around the perimeter. If you are inside, dissolve the salt in spring water and anoint all the door and window frames, moving clockwise around the house. Visualize your construct of protection while doing this.

Your home is now blessed with the protection spirit you have created.

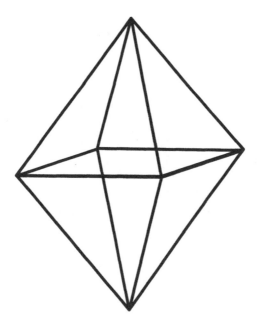

Figure 11. Octahedron

CHAPTER TWELVE
MAKING THE CONNECTION TO THE HIGHER SELF

THE VIEW FROM THE TOP FLOOR is spectacular. You can see far and wide, from horizon to horizon. All the marvels of the world are yours to gaze at, from the mountains to the night stars, but the people on the ground look like specs. They are moving around, but can you make out what they are doing? Probably not. However, if your best friend called and said he would be out front waiting for you, you would recognize his car pulling up. You would identify him and what he was doing. Although your friend can't see you, he knows you are there and can buzz up and tell you he is has arrived.

The higher self is has a similar penthouse view. It will yell out from the top floor if it sees a car heading toward you. If you are not listening, or do not recognize the higher self's unique voice, you will not hear the warning. The higher self has a linear advantage as well as a spatial advantage. Like other spirit allies, it is not bound by our sense of chronological time. It gives guidance based on possible futures and pasts.

At times the higher self can seem so far removed from the conscious you, it feels distant. But if you keep in contact with your higher self by simply being aware of it, it will connect and communicate with you more easily. The connection is like phoning ahead to check in before you do something.

Working with the higher self can be the easiest and the most dif-ficult aspect of spirit work. Higher selves are intimidating because they are the fully conscious and divine aspect of our being. They show us our potential to be as spiritual, loving, and balanced as any of our guides, guardians, teachers, and deities.

When my students work on connecting to the higher self, those who had no luck contacting spirit guides usually have spectacular results. Now they understand what other people are talking about when they get guidance. They find the inner voice they always had, thinking it was internal dialogue, but hear the special tone of their own voice that is their higher self. Those who already work with other spirit allies can have a marginal experience with their higher self, connecting only in a vague and unconscious way. Both experi-ences are good. Neither experience is better than the other. Those drawn to work only with spirit guides have something important and specific to learn from these guides. Those working with their higher self are working on their own self-relationship. The contact can come in the form of direct messages or by following your intu-ition. Spirit work and higher-self connections are not mutually exclusive. You can work with both. I do.

A modern trend many spiritual seekers have noticed is that the more you work with the higher self, the less your guides will be around. You are your own highest authority and best guide and guardian. Their goal is to help you see that and connect to your potential.

I have not personally noticed any shortage of spirits, however, since I keep on "bumping into" so many who are interested in help-ing the evolution of Earth. Many great changes are taking place, and beings from all levels want to be in on them. Eventually, if our goal is to create a true golden age with lasting peace on Earth, then we will all start living our higher self. We will continually act from this higher place of being.

The process of living your higher self is gradual and comes from your own conscious choices. Some people erroneously believe living your higher self is giving away all control to a higher, beneficent being. The thought excites some and scares others. Individuals who do not want to be responsible easily give up their choices and thereby their own personal evolution. On the other end of the spectrum, people fear giving up any control and do not want to trust in the universe and Great Spirit. I find the middle path is the healthy one.

For now, I speak with my higher self much like I do with other guides. Ceremonial magicians call this "Knowledge and Conversation of the Holy Guardian Angel." Your highest aspect takes on a spirit form to speak to you. Some call this your "Mighty I AM Presence" from the name God told to Moses, "I AM THAT I AM." We are each a part of that one spirit. The words "I AM" are used in many wonderful affirmations.

For me, the higher self usually appears formless and within me, but other times it is separate, as a great starry being of swirling galaxies and fiery suns. It gave me my true name, a translation of a name Mother Gaia calls me. Sometimes I feel my higher self over-shadowing me, residing within my physical body. It reminds me to work more through my love and honesty. I do not get a lot of direct guidance from my higher self. My guidance often comes in the form of a burst of intuition. These intuitive events are a reminder to con-sciously choose to live my higher self.

The higher self most often uses the lower self, the unconscious, to communicate with you. The unconscious exchanges your mes-sages through intuition, dreams, and ceremony.

Use Exercise 26 only when connecting to the higher self. The higher self has a unique relationship to us and we need unique tech-niques to achieve contact.

EXERCISE 26 – HIGHER-SELF CONNECTION

❶ Do Exercise 11, Pillar of Light.

❷ Visualize a beam of light extending out from the bottom of your spine running deep into the earth and completely surrounded by the pillar of light. This cord grounds you to Earth.

❸ Visualize a beam of light extending from the crown of your head up into the sky, completely surrounded by the pillar of light. This cord reaches up to your higher self.

❹ Intend to connect to your higher self and communicate with the highest aspect of yourself. Welcome it in.

❺ You might see a visual or just feel a presence with you. Welcome your higher self. Ask it any questions you have. Ask it what it may need of you.

❻ Thank your higher self and ask it to return to wherever it should be for your highest good. You do not have to stop the pillar of light or the cords of light. When you return to normal consciousness, they fade from your awareness.

If you do not receive a verbal communication, that is perfectly normal. Each experience is unique. Answers can come in your intuition or through external circumstances. Pay particular attention to your dreams. The next step in working with your higher self is up to you. Everyone has a unique relationship. The higher self can guide you to a technique, book, or workshop that will strengthen your bond with it, such as ascension material, shamanism, or daily meditation. No one can tell you what is correct and good for you except you and your higher self.

CHAPTER THIRTEEN

INVOKING SPIRIT

CONNECTING WITH THE SPIRIT world is fairly easy, as you have seen. The lands beyond the veil are part and parcel of our nature. We are intimately linked. This is our heritage. By opening to our full self, psychic senses included, we open the doorway to the spirit world, the "second road," but the street runs both ways. Just as we can enter the spirit worlds, the spirits can enter the material realm.

◎ INTERFACES WITH SPIRIT◎

At times your allies feel almost physical. Like my first encounter with Spider, you can stare eyes wide open and still feel another presence touching you. The experience is very vivid because you are in an altered state. Even in these extreme cases, you usually do not think the spirit has precipitated a material body out of nothing. You tell yourself it is a trick of energy and light. And it is, but our solid, physical bodies are also a trick of energy and light. The atoms and molecules forming our bodies are mostly empty space. The particles are not solid. They are energy and information, orbiting around empty space. Science cannot even pin down their locations, just probabilities of where they exist. These particles are fluctuations of energy. They give us the illusion we are solid. They trick us with our own light and energy. The spirit realms are not so different.

Ideally, we need an agent, an ally in the nonphysical realms to guide us through and work with us. Individuals can astrally project or shamanically journey to other realms without a guide, but the experiences tend to be deeper and safer if you are with some being who knows the ins and outs of the land. A good tour guide is always helpful in any land. Likewise, the spirit who wishes to inter-face with the material needs an agent, namely us.

Birth and Death

The first and most obvious way a spirit interfaces with the material world is through the incarnation process. The spirit is born into a body and its helper is of course the parents who create the body. We have all done this process before and we might all do it again if we so choose. Birth is one of the more permanent ways a spirit comes into the world.

The death and birth processes are remarkably similar. Both involve the exchange of spirit. So many people on Earth fear the death process, I wonder if the birth exchange is viewed with the same emotion on the other side of the veil. Although a multidimen-sional spirit is purposely forgetting its higher aspects and the nature of the universe, this being does so to be born and play the wonder-ful games life has to offer.

When we die, the spirit or soul disconnects from the body. The true essence seeks a return home. Spiritual mystery schools, partic-ularly Egyptian mysteries, claim the spiritual body, or Ka, stays for approximately three days inside or around the body. The journey then continues to the next life. In modern times, I do not find three days a hard and fast rule. Every experience is unique. Perhaps our feeling the presence of the departed at a funeral home or during a wake, funeral, or other passing rite is the manner in which the being stays close to its body, or more importantly, its family, until the soul is prepared for the transition.

Along with mystery teaching, we have modern near death experiences (NDEs) and past-life research indicating a guide or master leads or greets the deceased in a tunnel, filled with light, leading to the spirit realms. Joyful reunions occur with other departed family members, friends, and loved ones. The spirit undergoes a decompression period, unwinding, sharing experiences, and excitedly exploring the new world. The decompression is followed by a review of the past life, the games played, and lessons learned. The process seems very linear, but remember, this information is brought back by ordinary people, resuming linear life. The experiences must be remembered and related in a certain way to be understood. From that point, new games can be planned and experiences chosen. The cycle can begin again with birth or lead to a whole new environment and set of experiences. If the spirit decides to return to physical life, it assumes all the possibilities and limitations of the physical world, starting another grand game.

The other interfaces with spirit in this chapter are less common and involve a more conscious intent with our own spirit allies. By invoking spirit, we invite them to participate directly in the material world.

◎ OVERSHADOWING ◎

Overshadowing is simply a temporary blend of you and your ally. A spirit ally blends its energy with yours unconsciously. Imagine your guide standing behind you, looking over your shoulder like a teacher or helpful friend. Advice is given only when needed and in a way that will help you come to the conclusion yourself. Overshadowing is not like the boss standing over the assistant, dictating a letter. The effort is joint, but primarily yours. The spirit ally is there for assistance and encouragement and to provide what is needed. Together you are tapping your collective knowledge, wisdom, and experience. Most do not realize their allies are even there.

The overshadowing experience happens quite naturally and unconsciously. The guide knows when to be with you, as prompted by your higher self. Sometimes you need to be alone. Now that I understand the process better, I can specifically ask to be overshadowed by the ally most appropriate to me. When I am in session with anyone, doing healing work, tarot counseling, guid-ed meditation, or past-life work, I feel one or more of my guides overshadowing me. They lend support to situations I have no direct experience with. Sometimes they supply the right words or information a client needs to hear. They do the same thing when I run a class. I feel their presence, particularly Macha's, behind me, guiding me, but she is not controlling me or ordering me. The blend is gentle.

When I work on a book, or other metaphysical material, I ask to be connected to the appropriate guides. I actually create a con-nection with the purpose to write clearly and truthfully. Many of my guides participate in the connection, and when necessary over-shadow me. They will "pop" in when their expertise is needed.

Even with this connection, no one is dictating the book to me. I will write something, almost trancelike, then read it and wonder, "Where did that come from? I didn't know that. Is it true?" Then the appropriate guide will tell me that I intuitively knew the infor-mation but it helped put it into form. Then we will discuss it for a bit and I will add to it, answering the questions I had in the text. I experiment and play with the information to make sure it fits. The process starts as a sentence or two, but can be expanded into a chapter. Many spirituality authors work with their allies this way, tapping ancient wisdom now ready to be reclaimed.

This overshadowing exercise is one of the easiest in the book. Pick a time when you think you could use the support from your team. The situation could be a confrontation with someone in your family or a meeting with your boss. If you do any type of metaphysical work, that is a great avenue too. Before entering any of these situations, try the following exercise and see how it changes the experience.

E_XERC_I_SE 2 7 – OVERSHADOWING

❶ Take a few deep, relaxing breaths. Ask out loud or silently for any spirit ally who is correct and good for you now, coming in perfect love and trust, to overshadow you and aid you through this situation.

❷ Allow your allies' energy to overshadow yours and give you support.

❸ When the situation is complete, thank your allies for the help and ask them to end the overshadowing process.

Did you notice anything different in the situation or feel a presence? Sometimes it is very subtle but results in a greater self-confidence or awareness. You will find helpful words coming out of your mouth that you did not know you had. Usually direct guidance is sparse, since it would be difficult to listen to the guidance and work directly with others, particularly if they are unaware or unsupportive of your spirit work.

◎ ASSUMING GODFORMS ◎

Working with godforms, the archetypes of mythic deities, is a long-standing practice. Basically, you ask the energy of the deity to be present in you. Your consciousness does not leave, but becomes temporarily melded with the archetype. You assume the attributes of the deity, taking on its presence and persona. People around you with sensitivity recognize the change immediately. If you invoke a war god, you become more aggressive. When assuming a love goddess, you could become more sensual and sexual.

At first, you invoke deities by imagining yourself with their qualities and feeling them flood into your body. The process starts like playacting, but quickly becomes much more serious. Your thoughts change in one of two ways. You start having the thoughts of the archetype and your inner witness notices you are quite literally not yourself, or you have a very direct, conscious internal dialogue with the new consciousness entering you. The two voices in your mind, your little angel on the right shoulder and devil on the left become you and the deity. One voice is solely your own distinct conscious-ness and the other is the godform. You play out the same type of internal dialogue you would when making a decision, but this is lit-erally a conversation.

My first experience with this process was in witchcraft. During ritual, the priestess invokes and embodies the Goddess aspect and the priest embodies the God. Often, as the high priest in many ritu-als, I helped embody and guide the masculine god force in the ritu-als. Through a symbolic act of union, using a chalice and blade, the two energies of creation are brought together, like sperm and egg, and shared in the circle. The magic circle is truly a celebration of life in all aspects.

When I invoked the God aspect, grand and glorious, I got only hints and shades of His power. There is much love and energy in this act, but not a lot of personality and individuality. However, I felt connected to everyone and everything, inside the circle and out.

Soon I started experimenting with other godforms, in and out of ritual. The experience was very different. As a proponent of modern shamanism, I find dance clubs are one of the most trance-inducing rituals available. My partner and I experimented invoking some of the more "fun" godforms while dancing. I worked with Dionysus, god of wine and ecstasy, and Erzulie, a Voodoo loa. My partner called upon trickster gods like Loki and Raven. We had a great time, and it was definitely an interesting experience. The feel-ing of another presence inside you evokes external qualities in your body. We moved differently than we did without the godforms. We felt differently. We were different.

You can use these techniques to invoke the qualities and aid of the deities in your belief system. If you are shy and need to be fierce, invoke the dark goddess Kali. If you need confidence, wis-dom, and ingenuity, ask Pallas Athene to be part of you. When working on poetry, invoke a bardic god like Taliesin or the patron of the bards, Cerridwen. If you want children and have difficulty conceiving, invoke fertility and virility godforms like Demeter and Pan, respectively. Any quality, trait, or energy you need can be found in one of the mythic archetypes.

Ultimately you are in control of your body, and your visitor is like a houseguest. You are solely responsible for your actions and the actions of any being you bring through you. Only a small portion of these divine beings resides in you, a spark. They bring you a taste of their personality and light.

Do research and decide on what godform you wish to invoke before doing this exercise. Do a shamanistic journey or meditation to meet this being and introduce yourself before invoking it. Invoking beings you do not know is asking for trouble. You should always call before you come to someone's house, unless you know her really well. As in the material world, be polite to your spiritual guests.

EXERCISE 28 – ASSUMING GODFORMS

❶ Do Exercise 1 to reach a meditative state. Do any of the protective exercises you feel drawn to do.

❷ Say, "I ask to invoke the power of [name of chosen deity here] within me, in a manner correct and for my highest good, harming none. If it is not for my highest good, I ask that this invocation not occur."

❸ Allow the experience to happen. Look to the changes in your body and mind. Speak with this deity. It may be melded with you or capable of independent speech. Have fun with it, working with the powers and traits you invoked.

❹ When the experience is finished, thank the being for joining you. As a sign of respect, you can later burn incense or a candle in the deity's honor.

⑤ Make and speak the intention, "I release all that does not serve," three times. This releases any unwanted or harmful energies you may have picked up on your experience.

◎ CHANNELING ◎

Channeling is the act of getting information, for yourself or others, by conversing with a nonphysical being. The people opening themselves up to this information are opening or switching on a channel, like a television station. Usually questions are asked and answered. You can channel any spirit, even those not intimately connected to you, if you allow it, and you can channel spirit guides or your higher self. Entities you are channeling can take the role of spirit guide. Some do not distinguish between channeled entities and traditional spirit guides.

Channeling comes in two basic forms, conscious channelers and full-body channelers. Conscious channelers are in full control of their body and they repeat the message as given to them by the entity they are channeling. Full-body trance channelers relinquish control of their body, letting the spirit take over and speak through them. The spirit assumes control over motor functions or at least the speech centers. The channeler's consciousness either moves to the background or leaves entirely, possibly switching places with the consciousness of the entity. Many trance channelers have to record their sessions and be asked questions by other people because they remember nothing of the exchange when their consciousness returns to dominance.

With these two forms of channeling, we start the inevitable debate about which is better. Which one works for you? That is my answer: Full-body channels often feel there is no other way to go, and only by allowing the entity full access will your ego step aside and give a true message. All other channelings are tainted, filtered through the channel's ego. Full-body bypasses the ego.

Conscious channelers wonder why you would let a being without a physical body have control of yours. Have they had a human body before? Do they know how to take care of it? Could their own energy damage your body now? Why would they need to take over the body just to answer a question? Conscious channelers see the body as identified with the ego, so when a being takes on a body, they actually take on part of the ego, sometimes absorbing the speech patterns of their host. Listening to celestial beings with a Boston or English accent strikes me as very funny, but it happens. Conscious channelers can do a blend of energies, bringing their guide through, but not relinquishing control, like a more intense form of overshadowing.

Shamanic practitioners perform an aspect of channeling when, speaking in a trance state, they bring messages back from other-world beings. The shamanic approach differs from modern channeling since the shaman appears to go to the being instead of the spirit coming to them. Location, however, is a matter of perspective.

Discernment is paramount in any channeler's life. You must trust the entity you call. If you trust the being and know what techniques work for you, then use them. Becoming a channeler is a calling, much like any vocation, and should be entered only with a strong sense of self and a serious commitment to the work and the message being brought through to the world. Channeling is not for everybody.

◎ SHAPE-SHIFTING ◎

Shape-shifting does not actually invoke a spirit into your body like the other methods. Shape-shifting is the art of altering your own energy and spirit form to assume other characteristics and abilities. The most common form of shape-shifting is changing your human energy field into that of an animal, particularly your totem animal. Through this transformation, you assume the abilities and talents of the animal. You receive its medicine. Magical transformations are common in the otherworld, particularly in the Celtic tradition.

This shift of form and function occurs mainly in two ways. The first and easiest way makes people feel somewhat silly. You close your eyes and act out what you are shifting into, like an animal. Shamans call this dancing your animal. If you are bird, spread your arms like wings. When shifting into a wolf, growl on all fours. Imagine how your animal would act, and do it. Imagine you are the animal. Drumming music can help you get into this state. As you act things out, your energy conforms to your wishes. You feel different. Good actors shift their form when acting, assuming the energy of the character they play. They shape-shift without knowing it.

The meditative journey, where you are openly perceiving energy while traveling in a shamanic otherworld, is the second method. Your astral self is quite mutable. There you intend yourself to change shapes. If you assume a bird form, your arms will feel like they are transforming to wings, growing feathers, while your legs retract into bird claws. You then find yourself flying. When traveling the other-worlds, you might find your own shape naturally shifting. When entering a dark hole, suddenly you feel like a rabbit, gopher, or ant. Transformation is a natural part of the shamanic experience. Do not fight it. Flow with it. Shape-shifting is not limited to your totem animal, but your power animal is a great place to start.

E$_X$ERC$_I_S$E 29 – SHAPE-SHIFTING WITH YOUR TOTEM

❶ Start Exercise 14, Finding Your Power Animal.

❷ Once you have contacted your power animal, intend to shift into a similar shape and become the same animal. Imagine your astral body in the other world shifting. What appears to be blood, bone, and muscle flows like water until you are in your new form.

❸ Ask your power animal to guide you in this new shape. Follow where it leads.

❹ When you are ready, return your shape back into human form. You will not get stuck as an animal. Will it and it happens.

❺ Return to the trunk of the world tree, the middle world, by the same tunnel you came down.

❻ Return your perceptions to the room. Make and speak the

intention, "I release all that does not serve," three times. This releases any unwanted or harmful energies you may have picked up on your journey.

Soon you will start acting and sounding like your power animal and even thinking like it. Sometimes the shift is just "skin" deep or it can reach a more psychological level. At this deeper level the medicine of the animal and its lessons start to take root. Shape-shifting into your power animal is an excellent way to understand and identify with it and its real world counterparts. Learn your medicine and embrace the animal within you.

◎ Riding ◎

In Voodoo, which blends tribal magic of Africa with Catholicism, the gods–called "loa," meaning "laws"–are invited into the body, granting them full-body control. The consciousness of the individual takes a backseat to the loa. Ecstatic dancing and drumming allow the individual to maintain the necessary mind state for such an event to occur. The loa spirit is said to be "riding" the priest, like one would ride a horse. The horse still has a mind of its own, but the direction is guided completely by the loa. Actually, the loa usually rides the ritual participants more often than it rides those conducting and controlling the ceremony.

Riding is similar to many of the techniques here. Many of the loa are animal-like combinations of tribal spirits blended with and disguised as Catholic saints. Damballah Wedo is a snake god, and when riding a person, causes him to exhibit serpentine characteristics, like swaying and slithering on the ground. These movements facilitate the trance state according to modern European Seith magicians who practice the art of swaying and shaking. If you did not know what was occurring, you might think it a form of shape-shifting.

Since loa are godforms, riding is similar to invoking, but you are relinquishing a lot of control to the godform. This lack of control is reminiscent of full-body trance channeling, but most trance channels

I have encountered tend to be very intellectual. They sit around and answer questions in quite a Western civilized manner. Riding could simply be a more tribal form of full-body trance channeling.

◎ POSSESSION ◎

Possession by some evil being is the fear so many people have when dabbling with spirit work. They expect a scene right out of *The Exorcist*, with heads spinning around and pea soup flying. While I admit to the possibility, the occurrence is much rarer than most people think.

We are sovereign over our bodies and experiences, and something cannot take that control unless we let it. If we all cocreate our own reality and experiences for our higher good, then a being would not be able to possess us unless on some level we allow it. The more we are consciously in harmony with our higher aspects, the less likely this will happen.

Using the techniques outlined in this book will not lead to possession. The protective measures are some of the first things taught. They involve light because light burns away impurities and harm. One of my teachers tells me it is not enough to use light, but we must be the light. Then nothing can harm us. We are light beings and have to acknowledge and accept that mantle.

If you are afraid of possession, the first thing you need to do is make yourself feel more comfortable and face the fear. Ask yourself where the fear is rooted. It could come from this life or a past-life pattern. Those of us interested in magic, psychic talents, and spirits in this life probably have past-life links to them. Ask your guides. If you are not comfortable with a certain techniques, do not use them. They are not for everybody. This is a survey of many different techniques, cultures, and outlooks. If one fits you better than the others, stick with what works. If the idea of invoking spirit into your body, even a simple archetype, bothers you, then do not do it. If you do not want to be a full-body trance channel, never attempt it.

CHAPTER FOURTEEN

WORKING WITH SPIRITS

IF YOU SUBSCRIBE TO BELIEF IN SPIRIT allies with an independent existence beyond our imagination, then it stands to reason they are available for anyone. Spirits are not exclusive to any one individual. They work with many. Traditionally you need only a spirit's name or awareness to call it into your sacred space. Medieval texts have lists of names for magicians to use, including spirits, demons, angels, genies, and gods. If one knew the name of the spirit, then he had the power to call and bind it. Now we know there are plenty of spirits around us, and certain ones are correct and good for us to call. They want to help us, so I would chose the eager helpers first.

◎ OUR INDIVIDUAL ALLIES ◎

We each have individual allies to guide and guard us. We resonate with them, perhaps from past lives, present spiritual choices, or future needs. They know us best and have been charged, either self-chosen or by the higher powers. With their higher view, they see the entire forest of our lives, when we are stuck on looking at a particular tree. Allies probably have a better idea where our path is heading.

When we are in harmony with them, communicating with our guides and higher aspects, we can reap their wisdom. When we ignore their calls and signs, problems are aggravated. Their wisdom makes life easier in the end.

◎ AIDING OTHERS SPIRITUALLY ◎

If you choose to aid others on spiritual issues or practice a meta-physical discipline, it is easy to think you have the higher view. If you feel you are farther along on a path when compared to someone just spreading her wings, you can easily feel like her guide or spiritual ally. Help, advice, and genuine skill are great, but remember you do not have the perspective beyond space and time that a guide may have. No matter how advanced, wise, or spiritual you are, you are still human. This means you have an ego and a limited view. The best way to help people is to help them find their own guidance and inner knowing. Feed a starving man and do a good deed, but if you teach him how to fish, bake, or hunt, you feed him for a lifetime. If you help someone to tap in to her own spiritual advice, you are spiritually nourishing this person with an inexhaustible source of aid for life.

I started aiding people with personal issues using intuitive skills and tarot cards. Soon I was asked to join a psychic fair. I found myself giving professional card readings and learning early on that although I helped clarify situations and point out potentials, I did not have the answers they were seeking. People discover their own answers. Sessions like this help people figure things out, even if they are not interested in spirit allies or divine guidance.

Healers are in the same situation. Metaphysicians work not only with the body, like doctors, but with the entire being, including emotions, mind, and spirit–all are connected. When doing a healing session for a specific illness or injury, the issues creating it float to the surface. The healer finds himself in the position of counselor, not energy worker. For those with natural empathy, listening skills develop quickly, but the situations can still be difficult without fur-ther training.

Do not confuse your personal view with higher guidance. Your road is only for you, but your experiences and techniques can be a great help for others. As a witch, my spirituality forced me to confront a lot of my own self-esteem and emotional issues. In essence, witchcraft helped me solve a lot of my problems, but witchcraft is not the answer for all my clients. They get valuable information from my experiences in witchcraft, including meditation, past-life regression, psychic abilities, healing, and empowerment rituals, and then seek their own path starting with those topics, rather than witchcraft specifically.

The benefit of working in healing professions is being a vehicle for the guidance of others. Set aside your own beliefs and attachments, your ego, and become an open channel for higher guidance. From your personal experiences, you have gathered and developed the skills necessary to commune with the spirit world for yourself and others.

◎ Inviting Allies into Your Work ◎

When working in client or class situations, be open to your own allies. Invoke them before a session. Enter a light meditative state. If you have clients open to these concepts, do it out loud and make a ritual out of it. For healing sessions, invoke a healing field, magic circle, or your own ritual. Most times it is best to do these things privately, particularly if you are in a quieter discipline like massage therapy or traditional counseling. Invoke your allies privately, but put out the intention you would like their help in a manner correct and good for yourself and client.

Ask to be open to your clients' allies. If your allies work best with you, and have information you need, then your clients' allies must have information and support for them. Many people have not developed the skills needed to communicate with their guides and may never develop them. Sometimes people listen through intuition, but they lack the direct communication. Their guides would love to get a message through. At appropriate times, you can be the medium through which the message comes.

You probably will not know the names of your clients' spirit guides, so asking to be open to their allies is enough. They do have independent existence and framework, even though each person may interact with them uniquely.

My flower essence practitioner asks for help from my guides in choosing essences correct and good for me. His method is the pendulum, but he is also clairaudient and clairsentient. During one session, he commented on the spirits he perceived, telling me that I had two guides who did not always see eye to eye. One is more direct and masculine; the other is feminine and gentle in approach. He then accurately described Llan and Asha, the two guides I invoked to help me get the right essence combination before entering his office. I had not told him I worked with these guides and he never told me he usually asks for that kind of guidance. I was pretty impressed.

In another session, he described a woman with big, black, iridescent wings, standing behind me. I always picture Macha, the crow goddess, behind me, with her wings outstretched. She sometimes wraps them around me like a cloak of feathers. For me, such an experience was one of the greatest arguments against spirit allies being a figment of the mind, having only personal significance. As I had more of these experiences, I really started to believe in their independent existence. The doubts dissolved away.

Years ago, I was driving home from work in a snowstorm. My partner, who works with Odin and his two ravens, Hugin and Munin, or Thought and Memory, asked the raven spirits to guide me home safely. While sitting in traffic, slowly inching up the icy highway and completely unaware of his intention, I got the impression of big black birds. They did not feel like crows or Macha, but something else entirely. They felt nonthreatening and I knew they were not physical, but I soon lost the image in my snowy frustration. I had traffic and ice to worry about. Later that night my partner told me about his petition to the ravens and I was amazed.

I have been inviting allies into my work more frequently, and have been aware of other people's personal allies at workshops, in sessions, and generally out and about when I feel like looking with second sight. It happens most frequently during Reiki and tarot sessions. I feel or see extra sets of hands around the person lying on the massage table. They show me places to specifically work or symbols to use in healing. Messages often come through to help their emotional healing.

In card sessions, it is almost like I have opened a door of light behind my client and a crowd of allies gather around to give advice. They can, along with my own allies, help me interpret the cards or give me direct information as it pertains to the reading. Sometimes they have a specific message that makes absolutely no sense to me, but I trust them to have meaning for my client, and usually they do. Messages that do not make sense feel the clearest, because I know that my ego is in no way involved. Once I was told to pass along the message, "remember your dog," and I know I would not normally think of that phrase. I got a call from that client a few days later telling my how the dog turned out to be significant in the healing process.

Since I have opened myself up to working with other people's allies when necessary, some allies seek me out. These rare visitors come with special messages or ask me to teach someone a few simple skills to make their own connection process easier. If you introduce someone to the skills of spirit work, or pass along a book like this, you help her connect to her own guidance naturally. You empower her rather than make her dependent on you.

Try the next exercise with a friend who would be open to it, preferably one who is also studying these techniques and can return the favor by reversing roles with you.

EXERCISE 30 – CONNECTING TO OTHER ALLIES

❶ Sit down quietly with your partner or client. You will be speaking to his spirit ally, but it is important to initially have a physical presence to make the connection. You can connect again without the physical presence.

❷ Do Exercise 1 to reach a meditative state. Do any of the protective exercises you feel drawn to do.

❸ Say, "I ask to communicate with the spirit ally of [state the person's name], in a manner correct and for our highest good, harming none." If your partner is aware of his own ally's name, and you wish to communicate with that specific ally, you can substitute that name.

❹ Allow the experience to happen. It is different for everyone. Your psychic senses, including sight, sound, or gut-level intuition, open.

❺ Communicate with this spirit being. Ask it any questions on behalf of your partner. Either vague impressions or specific messages occur. Go with the experience, however it unfolds.

❻ Thank this spirit ally for its time and for communicating with you.

❼ Make and speak the intention, "I release all that does not serve," three times. This releases any unwanted or harmful energies you may have picked up on your experience.

Working with other people's spirit allies is a great talent to possess, helping you to help them. If you have difficulty connecting like this, do not fear. Your own allies will help you translate if they can. Do not despair if you are introduced to a guide your partner has never met. The reason you might be connecting with that unknown guide is because your partner has a block to the issues this guide teaches. We all have more allies than we consciously realize.

◎ THE NEW AGE ◎

As we enter the twenty-first century, with all our potential disasters and miracles alike, our true hope of embodying the golden age is to work in partnership with all beings, including spirits. Spirits of all kinds, from the animal, vegetable, and mineral worlds, are reaching out to us, strange as it seems. The choice is ours. Do we take their hands and re-create a heaven on Earth, or do we ignore them, as we have for the past several hundred years, and usher in an end?

The true New Age is not commercialized spirituality, but an age of expanded consciousness and honoring spirit. Through the simple act of honoring, we open our eyes to the true reality. We are all spirit. We already live in a spirit world. Everything is sacred. To survive we need to honor the spirit of all things, everywhere. We are connected, but they made the first moves toward love. To usher in the New Age, we need to start right at home, by honoring our fellow human beings, our environment, and our own spirit allies.

ANGELS

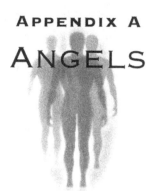

IN NO WAY CAN THIS BE A COMPLETE list of angels and angel hierarchies. Volumes have been written on this subject alone. The following is a simple list of known archangels and their correspondences. Many sources of angel lore are contra-dictory regarding the hierarchies, correspondences, and even spelling of their names. If interested in working with angels, do your own research into the topic and, most importantly, ask one.

Azreal: Angel of Death, separator of spirit from body, underworld guide, possible form of Raphael or Uriel

Camuel: Angel of Mars, war, love, compassion, forgiveness, strength, courage, protection, justice

Gabriel: Angel of Water and the Moon, messenger, herald, clarity, purification, emotional healing, change, paradise

Haniel: Angel of Venus, protection from evil, illumination, virtue, completion, harmony, innocence, beauty

Jophiel: Angel of the Torah (Law), mental powers, learning, edu-cation, companion of Metatron

Kafziel: Angel of Saturn, karma, chief aid to Gabriel

Metatron: Angel of Spirit, King of Angels, teacher, organization, link to the divine, enlightenment, companion of Jophiel

Michael: Angel of Fire, Sun, warrior, protector, keeper of the flaming sword, remover of evil, leader of the heavenly armies, courage, truth

Raphael: Angel of Air and Mercury, healer, protector of travelers, guide in the underworld, truth, abundance, success, honor, and contacting your guardian angel

Ratziel: Angel of Mysteries, secrets, divine wisdom, illumination, guidance

Uriel: Angel of Earth, bringer of knowledge, regeneration, releaser of fear, womb, death, growth, peace, salvation, thunder

Zadkiel: Angel of Jupiter, teacher of spirituality, violet flame, transmutation, tolerance, mercy

ASCENDED MASTERS AND COSMIC BEINGS

THIS IS A LIST OF CORRESPONDENCES for some of the most well-known ascended masters and cosmic beings currently working with people on Earth. Many more most likely exist. Some are associated with specific rays of light. You can learn more about these rays from *The Ascended Masters Light the Way* by Joshua David Stone. Since many of the masters have lived on Earth before or after their spiritual ascension, I have provided their possible previous incarnations, although many sources give conflicting information. Some recently deceased holy people, healers and activists thought to be ascended masters but not listed here are Paramahansa Yogananda, Dr. Usui, Mother Theresa, Ghandi, Madame Blavatsky, Edgar Cayce, and Peace Pilgrim.

Afra: First ascended master of Africa, rhythm of life, spirit

Alizor: Healer, medical aid

Ashtar: Ashatar Command, Galactic Federation

Buddha: He Who Is Awake, kindness, compassion, charity

Djwhal Khul: Esoteric teaching, information

El Morya: First Ray, red, will, power, action
Possible Previous Incarnations: Abraham, King Solomon, Melchior (of the Three Wise Men), King Arthur

Gwydion: The Man Who Changes, magic, shape-shifting, laughter

Hilarion: Fifth Ray, orange, science, New Age, prophecy, guide to the disappointed or disillusioned
Possible Previous Incarnations: Paul the Apostle

John the Apostle: Research, information, holistic therapy

Kahunda: Healing, medicine man
Possible Previous Incarnations: Appears as a mix of Native American, African, and Aboriginal healers

Kumeka: Eight Ray, higher cleansing
Possible Previous Incarnations: Never incarnated on Earth

Kuthumi: Second Ray, deep blue, sacred geometry, math, music, philosophy, love
Possible Previous Incarnations: Pythagoras, St. Francis of Assisi, Galileo, Shah Jahan

Lanto: Education, guide to teachers, learning, knowledge

Lorporis: Head of the healing teams

Luciar: Healer

Maha Chohan: Leadership, adding spirit to positions of power, mineral and crystal work

Marko: Galactic Federation, Saturn

Melchizedek: Magic, wisdom
Possible Previous Incarnations: King Melchizedek of Salem

Mother Mary: Healing, initiation, goddess energy
Possible Previous Incarnations: Isis, White Buffalo Woman, possibly Quan Yin

Nada: Remover of veils, helper of those who feel they were mislead by religion, truth

Pallas Athena: Counseling

Paul the Venetian: Fourth Ray, arts

Quan Yin: Karma, healing, children, compassion
   Possible Previous Incarnations: Mother Mary, White Buffalo Woman

Quetzalcoatl: Master of Life, Venus, civilization, art

Sananda: Sixth Ray, indigo, devotion, spirituality
   Possible Previous Incarnations: Jesus Christ, Adam, Enoch, Jeshua, Joshua, Joseph of Egypt

Sanat Kumara: Planetary Logos, avatars, Venus, evolution, manifestation

Serapis Bey: Third Ray, formerly Fourth Ray, white flame, arts, mental powers, angelic evolution
   Possible Previous Incarnations: Akhenaten

St. Germain: Seventh Ray, violet flame, civilization, Reiki, magic, transformation, healing
   Possible Previous Incarnations: Merlin, Samuel the Prophet, Joseph of Nazareth, Proclus the Philosopher, Christopher Columbus, Sir Francis Bacon

Thoth: Order of Melchizedek, sacred geometry, teaching
   Possible Previous Incarnations: Hermes Trismegistus

Vywamus: Higher Self of Sanat Kumara, breaker of misconceptions

Wontanna: Mother Earth, animals, nature healing, Native American teachings

PAGAN GODS

THE DEITIES FROM THE WORLD'S mythology are as diverse as the cultures of the world. Appendix C is an introductory list to some pagan gods and their correspondences. Each god and myth is much more complex than the correspondences given here. By studying the myths, you gain greater insight into the deity's nature and province. Notice the similarities of certain archetypal images across cultures. Since the Greek and Roman gods are often viewed as equivalent beings with different names, they are listed together when possible.

NAME	CULTURE	CORRESPONDENCES
Aphrodite/Venus	Greek/Roman	Goddess of love, sensuality, ecstasy
Apollo	Greek/Roman	Sun, fire, poetry, inspiration, sports, music, prophecy
Astarte/Ishtar	Babylonian	Queen of Heaven, love, relationships, power, mother, light

NAME	CULTURE	CORRESPONDENCES
Athena/Minerva	Greek/Roman	Wisdom, battle, strategy
Bel	Celtic	Young god of light, fire, purity, sexuality
Brid	Celtic	Triple goddess (maiden, mother, crone) of fire, poetry, smith work, healing
Cernunnos	Celtic	Horned god, master of the hunt, animals, wilderness
Cerridwen	Celtic	Moon mother, cauldron, crone, poetry, inspiration, art, transformation, bards
Chac	Mayan	Rain, vegetation, jungles, serpents
Dagda	Celtic	Good god, gentleness, wisdom, abundance, prosperity
Damballa Wedo	Voodoo/African	Snakes, serpents, sex, masculine force, nature, prophecy
Danu	Celtic	Earth goddess, harvest, cosmic mother
Demeter/Ceres	Greek/Roman	Goddess of grain, land, growing things

NAME	CULTURE	CORRESPONDENCES
Enlil	Sumerian	Earth and land, counselor to the gods
Erzulie	Voodoo/African	Love, relationships, scorned lovers
Freyja	Norse	Great Goddess, magic, seas, amber, nature
Gaia	Greek	Mother Earth, bounty, life, love, prophecy
Ganesha	Hindu	Elephant-headed, remover of obstacles, granter of luck, wisdom, writing
Gwydion	Celtic	Magic, shape-shifting, illusions
Hades/Pluto	Greek/Roman	Lord of the Dead, riches
Hecate	Greek/Roman	Triple goddess (maiden, mother, crone) of the crossroads, underworld, death
Hathor	Egyptian	Moon, cows, womb, sky, nature, happiness
Hermes/Mercury	Greek/Roman	Traveler, teacher, inventor, messenger, guide
Horus	Egyptian	Divine child, avenger, justice, Sun, falcons

Name	Culture	Correspondences
Isis	Egyptian	Motherhood, sorcery, resurrection, Moon, magic
Kali	Hindu	Black mother, death, karma, release
Loki	Norse	Mischief, fire, light, shape-shifting, trickster
Lugh	Celtic	Sun, grain, harvest, healing, magic, poetry, many-skilled one, golden light
Macha	Celtic	Mother, crone, crows, battle, protection
Marduk	Sumerian	King of the gods, creator, justice, keeper of cycles
Mictlantecutli	Aztec	Lord of the Dead, underworld, skeletons
Morigan	Celtic	Triple goddess (maiden, mother, crone) war, death, regeneration, underworld
Poseidon/Neptune	Greek/Roman	Sea, oceans, water, rivers, storms, safe travel by boat, collective unconscious
Odin/Wotan	Norse	Wanderer, magic, runes, madness, divine inspiration

NAME	CULTURE	CORRESPONDENCES
Osiris	Egyptian	Death, resurrection, underworld, fertility, life, immortality
Pan	Greek	Nature, animals, plants, frivolity, passion, lust, sexuality
Pele	Hawaiian	Volcanoes, fire, lava, passion, earth, creation
Persephone/ Proserpina	Greek/Roman	Underworld goddess, grain, death and resurrection, maidenhood
Quan Yin	Asian	Mother, compassion, love, and children
Quetzalcoatl	Mayan/Aztec	Feathered serpent, compassion, magic, light, creation, priesthood, wind, oceans, life
Ra	Egyptian	Sun, supreme god, creator, power, magic, justice
Selene	Greek	Moon, memories, sleep, magic
Shiva	Hindu	Dissolver of form, dance, magic, power
Thor	Norse	Thunder, lightning, storm, protection, justice

NAME	CULTURE	CORRESPONDENCES
Thoth	Egyptian	Scribe, teaching, magic, geometry
Tlazoteotl	Aztec	Underworld goddess, eater of filth, darkness
Zeus/Jupiter	Greek/Roman	Supreme god, lightning, protection, law, justice

POWER ANIMALS AND ANIMAL MEDICINE

POWER ANIMALS, TOTEMS, AND familiars are best experienced firsthand. This list gives a description of the medicine some of the more common animals bring.

Ant: Organization, group consciousness, community, patience, determination

Bear: Introspection, meditation, hibernation, solitude, retreat, intuition, womb

Beetle: Regeneration, death

Buffalo: Spirituality, sacredness, abundance, prosperity, balance

Bull: Virility, stamina, endurance, connection to Goddess, Moon, emotions, passion, comfort

Butterfly: Transformation, creativity, new ideas, talents, inner beauty

Cat: Moon, magic, instincts, intuition, otherworlds

Coyote: Trickster, illusions, magic, sense of humor

Crab: Security, family, protection

Crow: Shape-shifting, fascination, protection, spiritual law, change, reading the future

Deer: Compassion, love, gentleness

Dog: Loyalty, companionship, unconditional love

Dolphin: Sacred breath, rhythm, water, dreaming

Dragonfly: Seeing through illusions, romanticism, breaking delusions

Eagle: Travel, messages, signals, power, spirit, observation

Fox: Invisibility, camouflage, wind, fire, cunning

Frog: Water, singing, purification, environment, sensitivity

Goose: Warning, finding voice, travel

Horse: Power, shamanic worlds, journey

Lion: Family, leadership, royalty, responsibility

Lizard: Regeneration, paying attention to dream life

Mosquito: Removing fear, dealing with annoyance

Mouse: Sensitivity, scrutiny, blindness, organization, fear

Otter: Motherhood, children, care, play, feminine energy

Owl: Divination, magic, astral travel, wisdom, true sight

Rabbit: Manifesting harm, running away from fear

Ram: Courage, facing fear, bravery, obstinacy

Raven: Mysticism, magic, darkness, the void, creation, gods and goddesses, messages, travel

Salmon: Memory, return, homeland, giving to the next generation

Sea Horse: Fidelity, gender role reversals

Snake: Regeneration, shedding your skin, Earth connection, change, adaptation

Spider: Creativity, writing, overcoming fear

Squirrel: Preparing for future, gathering, storing

Swan: Inner beauty, coordination, grace

Turtle: Protection, Goddess, Earth, grounding, centering

Whale: History, keeping records, sound, telepathy, song

Wolf: Protection, family, teacher, sharing, knowledge

THE HERMETIC LAWS

THE HERMETIC LAWS ARE ANCIENT teachings about the universe from the mystery schools of Greece and possibly Egypt. Their fabled creator, Hermes Trismegistus, has faded into mythological obscurity, but the principles survive, probably best known in the *Kybalion,* a philosophical work credited to the Three Initiates. Since the principles are cited often in the discussion of the material and spiritual worlds, I have included a general overview here.

The Law of Mentalism: All things in existence are "creations of THE ALL" or thoughts in the divine mind. We are all one in the divine.

The Law of Correspondence: "As above, so below." Patterns repeat themselves on all scales imaginable. Microcosms and macrocosms are maps of each other. The inner and outer worlds are intimately connected.

The Law of Polarity: "Everything is dual; everything has poles; everything has its pair of opposites." One of the active forces of the universe is the attraction and repulsion between the sets of poles.

The Law of Vibration: "Nothing rests; everything moves; everything vibrates." With the discovery of the atom, science has proved this principle beyond a doubt.

The Law of Gender: "Gender is in everything; everything has its masculine and feminine principles." Everything and everyone contains a mixture of feminine attributes and masculine attributes.

The Law of Rhythm: "Everything flows in and out; everything has its tides." The universe works in cycles and patterns that repeat themselves, like the cycles of nature and the stars.

The Law of Cause and Effect: "Every cause has its effect; every effect has its cause." This law is similar to our modern belief that "every action has an equal and opposite reaction." Everything occurring has an effect on everything else. Events occurring now are effects of previous causes.

BIBLIOGRAPHY

Andrews, Ted. *Animal-Speak: The Spiritual & Magical Powers of Creatures Great and Small*. St. Paul, MN: Lewellyn, 1993.

Belhayes, Iris, with Enid. *Spirit Guides*. San Diego, CA: ACS Publications, 1986.

Black, Jason S., and Christopher S. Hyatt, P.h.D. *Urban Voodoo A Beginner's Guide to Afro-Caribbean Magic*. Tempe AZ: New Falcon Publications, 1995.

Cabot, Laurie. *Witchcraft As a Science, I and II*. Salem, MA, 1993. (class handouts and lecture notes)

Cabot, Laurie, with Tom Cowan. *Power of the Witch: The Earth, the Moon, and the Magical Path to Enlightenment*. New York: Delacorte, 1998.

Chopra, Deepak. *Magical Mind, Magical Body*. Chicago: Nightingale-Conant Corporation, 1990. Audiocassette.

Clow, Barbara Hand. *The Pleiadian Agenda: A New Cosmology for the Age of Light*. Santa Fe, NM.: Bear & Company, 1995.

Conway, D. J. *The Ancient & Shining Ones*. St. Paul, MN: Llewellyn, 1993.

Cooper, Diana. *A Little Light on Ascension*. Findhorn, Scotland: Findhorn Press, 1997.

Cowan, Tom. *Fire in the Head*. New York: HarperSanFrancisco, 1993.

Crowley, Vivianne. *Wicca, the Old Religion in the New Age*. San Francisco: The Aquarian Press, 1989.

Davidson, Gustav. *A Dictionary of Angels: Including the Fallen Angels*. New York: The Free Press, 1967.

Frissel, Bob. *Nothing in This Book Is True But It's Exactly How Things Are*. Berkeley, CA: Frog Ltd., 1994.

Guiley, Rosemary Ellen. *The Encyclopedia of Ghosts and Spirits*. New York: Facts On File, Inc., 1992.

———. *Harper's Encyclopedia of Mystical & Paranormal Experience*. New York: HarperSanFrancisco, 1991.

———. *The Encyclopedia of Witches and Witchcraft: Second Edition*. New York: Checkmark Books/Facts on File, 1999.

Harner, Michael. *The Way of the Shaman*. 3rd ed. New York: Harper Collins, 1990.

Hine, Phil. *Condensed Chaos*. Tempe, AZ: New Falcon, 1995.

Kenyon, Tom. *Sound Healing and the Inner Terrain of Consciousness*. Videocassette. Acoustic Brain Research and Big Dipper Productions. n.d.

Kenyon, Tom, and Virginia Essene. *The Hathor Material*. Santa Clara, CA: Spiritual Education Endeavors Publishing Company, 1996.

Kybalion, The: A Study of the Hermetic Philosophy of Ancient Egypt and Greece. The Three Initiates, eds. Kila, MT.: Kessinger Publishing, 1997.

Milner, Kathleen. *Reiki and Other Rays of Touch Healing*. Scottsdale, AZ.: self-published, 1995.

Myss, Caroline. *Anatomy of the Spirit: The Seven Stages of Power and Healing*. New York: Three Rivers Press, 1996.

Osborn, Kevin and Dana L. Burgess, Ph.D. *The Complete Idiot's Guide to Classical Mythology*. New York: Alpha Books, 1998.

Peschel, Lisa. *A Practical Guide to the Runes*. St. Paul, MN: Llewellyn Publications, 1991.

RavenWolf, Silver. *To Stir a Magick Cauldron*. St. Paul, MN: Llewellyn Publications, 1995.

Rei, Shakura. *Ascending Star.* 1999. www.ascending-star.com 3/1/99

Sams, Jamie, and David Carson. *Medicine Cards: The Discovery of Power Through the Ways of the Animals.* Santa Fe, NM: Bear & Company, 1998.

Sanchez, Victor. *The Teachings of Don Carlos.* Santa Fe, NM: Bear & Company, 1995.

Small Wright, Machaelle. *MAP: The Co-Creative White Brotherhood Medical Assistance Program.* Jeffersonton, VA: Perelandra, Ltd., 1994.

———. *Perelandra Garden Workbook: A Complete Guide to Gardening with Nature Intelligences.* Jeffersonton, VA: Perelandra, Ltd., 1987.

Smith, Gary. *Sacred Merkaba Techniques, Science of Inner Love & Light.* June 8, 2001. www.merkaba.org 5/25/99.

Stone, David Joshua. *The Ascended Masters Light the Way: Beacons of Ascension.* Sedona, AZ: Light Technology Publishing, 1995.

———. *The Complete Ascension Manual.* Sedona, AZ: Light Technology Publishing, 1994.

Thorsson, Edred. *Northern Magic: Mysteries of the Norse, Germans and English.* St. Paul, MN: Llewellyn Publications, 1992.

Weiss, Brian. *Many Lives, Many Masters.* New York: Simon & Schuster, 1988.

Whitcomb, Bill. *The Magician's Companion: A Practical & Encyclopedic Guide to Magical & Religious Symbolism.* St. Paul, MN: Llewellyn Publications, 1993.

Yin, Amorah Quan. *The Pleiadian Workbook: Awaking Your Divine Ka.* Santa Fe, NM: Bear & Company, 1996.